THE LOVED FORGIVE
THE FORGIVEN LOVE...

It Is Time

BY

MARILYN HUME

᰾ ◆ ᰾

It is Time

Copyright © 2008 - Marilyn Hume

www.bethbiri.com

Unless otherwise noted, all scriptures quotations are from the NEW AMERICAN STANDARD BIBLE (R), Copyright (C) 1960, 1962, 1963, 1968, 1971, 1972, 1973, 1975, 1977, 1995 by The Lockman Foundation. Used by permission.

Scripture quotations marked GW are taken from the God's Word, copyright © 1995 by GOD'S WORD to the Nations Bible Society. All rights reserved.

Scripture quotations marked *The Message* are taken from The Message: The Bible in Contemporary English, copyright © 1993, 1994, 1995, 1996, 2000, 2001, 2002. Used by permission of NavPress Publishing Group.

Scripture quotations marked NIV are taken from the The Holy Bible, New International Version. Copyright © 1973, 1978, 1984 by International Bible Society. Used by permission.

Scripture quotations marked NKJV are taken from the New King James Version of the Bible. Copyright © 1979, 1980, 1982 by Samas Nelson, Inc., Publishers. Used by permission.

Scripture quotations marked TLB are taken from The Living Bible, Kenneth N. Taylor, copyright © 1971 by Tyndale House Publishers, Inc. Used by permission. All rights reserved.

ISBN 978-1440495670

Dedication

I dedicate this book to all who long to love,
long to be free, and long to see
God's glory displayed in the earth.

CONTENTS

Foreword...

When someone asks me for a description of humility, I simply give them a definition that Marilyn once told me: agreement with God. When God says, "You are gifted in an area and this is an area of strength for you," it is pride that says, "No I'm not really that good." Humility says, "Ok, God, thank you for giving me this strength." Marilyn's life lives this message.

She has a strong prophetic gift, coupled with total submission and commitment to walking in meekness - strength under control. She has been and continues to be steadfast and faithful to the ministry which God has entrusted to her.

Marilyn Hume is a marvelous equipper and facilitator of people discerning the voice of the Lord. The manner with which she trains people to courageously follow the leadership of the Holy Spirit is a lesson in meekness. Her tremendous gift in moving in prophetic ministry, and releasing others to do so, is only exceeded by her character and willingness to submit to leadership. Moving in the prophetic is often challenging, as one sees where God wants to take the church compared to the church in its present condition. That tension often breeds frustration and "edges" in the lives of those who wrestle with visions not yet realized. For over 20 years I have watched this mighty woman of God walk that tension with incredible character, balance and poise. She continues to keep her heart supple in the midst of difficult issues. I know that you will be challenged and blessed by all she has to say and teach.

The privilege of learning from, and walking alongside, this tremendous warrior is forever a lesson in the kindness of God.

Roll up your sleeves, prepare your heart, and walk with Christ to be upgraded through some practical insights from a woman I know walks with Jesus every day!

— Jason Albelo, Senior Pastor
East Hill Church, Gresham, Oregon

Thanks...

To my husband Doug who has little laugh wrinkles around his eyes. He has shown me the eyes of my Heavenly Father. Life with you is good!

To my mom and dad who exposed me at an early age to the love of God. Mom, you continue to love me. Thanks for who you are!

To my children, who have graciously allowed me to share openly and forgiven the mistakes I've made in raising them, and to my grandchildren who are such a joy to my heart! May God's blessings rest upon you to a thousand generations!

To my brother and sisters, family, friends, and co-workers who got to practice how to love with me. One day we might get it right! You have blessed my life in so many ways!

To youth workers, pastors, evangelists, ministers, and teachers, too many to mention, who taught me truth from God's Word, and made it alive. You laid a wonderful foundation, and have continued to build into my life!

To my mother-in-law, who sent me the tape, and Jerry Cook who preached a sermon on forgiveness that forever impacted my life.

To difficult people who have spurred me to grow in ways that would have otherwise been impossible. I am deeply indebted to you!

To all those who helped edit this material and gave me wonderful feedback. Karen Kolzow saw the humble beginnings, and encouraged me to be real about my emotions. My husband Doug suffered gracefully through my hours, days, and weeks of sitting on the couch writing and revising in my off-work hours, and provided excellent input and editing skills. Connie Fort, Sue Payne and her aunt, LaVeta Thompson, read my first drafts and gave me honest but very gracious evaluations about what was good and what wasn't working. Bob Hunter gave valuable insight from a different theological background, and helped me word some of the Points to Ponder more effectively. My sister, Naomi Fields, used her years of professionally proofing theses for graduate school students to give me some necessary technical adjustments a few revisions ago. I hope I remember everything you said! Michael Cohen, an Englishman, now from Israel, who I met in Korea, helped me clarify some of the Hebrew and Old Testament concepts. Isn't it amazing how God connects people around the world? My friend Ruth Swaim, as well as many others, gave me tremendous moral and spiritual support in the process. You all encouraged me to not give up, and helped me say what I wanted to say!

To all those who said God told them to pray for me and did at crucial times on the journey.

To Ted Roberts, Jason Albelo, and the wonderful pastors and people of East Hill Church, who have provided me with an atmosphere to grow, loved me and modeled God's love through your lives and actions. And Arlin Hill who encouraged me to dream again. I am!

To Jesus who makes it all possible!

Thanks!

Marilyn Hume

Introduction

When I was fifteen the church my family attended was going through very difficult times, as people I loved were accusing one another of unthinkable sins. Many were offended and left the church. It would have been easy for me to become embittered toward church and God and walk away, but the Lord had another plan.

One night my family went to a special meeting about thirty miles from our home town. I don't remember who spoke or what was said during the service, but I remember very clearly what happened afterwards.

An unknown man I recognized from other meetings approached me and said, "I don't know what you're going through, but I feel God wanted me to tell you to keep your eyes on Jesus, not on people."

I have since wondered what went through his head beforehand. Maybe he thought it was such a simple word that it was hardly worth mentioning. But I am so thankful he was obedient to the little impression that came into his heart. His word has helped me many times when I could have easily become bitter toward others because of their judgments, actions or attitudes. It's been a lifelong lesson for me.

I have seen many other young people struggle with bitterness and walk down roads of destruction. Marriages have been destroyed, and friends and families ripped apart. I have observed highly gifted and anointed men and women of God become prisoners of war and missing in action from the plans and purposes of God because they allowed a little wound to fester until it became a poison permeating their lives, disillusioning other believers, ruining churches, and making a mockery of the name of Christ in the world.

You may be one who has been wounded by the judgments or actions of others and currently struggle with bitterness and resentment, or you may want to help others get set free from their inner prisons. In either case I believe this book may help you.

It is a result of years of sitting at the feet of awesome men and women of God, personal observation and painful experience, quiet conversations with friends, revelation from God's word, and encounters with the Holy Spirit. The basic message could be summed up in a few statements or scriptures that, if you've followed Jesus for any time at all, would be familiar to you. We all know we should forgive. After all, Jesus said, "If you do not forgive you will not be forgiven." However, I have found it is much easier to obey a command when I understand the reason or heart behind the person giving it. I don't think it's just because I am rebellious. In the past I have been obedient to those who didn't have my best interest at heart, so sometimes it is not easy to trust again.

I suspect I am not alone in this struggle. Therefore, I have tried to communicate God's heart, nature and love for us, even while dealing with the difficult issues of judgments and unforgiveness. I certainly do not cover everything that could be said — I simply invite you to see through my lens. My desire is that we would come face to face with the Living God, get unstuck from where we are, learn to love as He loves, step into His full plans and purposes for us, and see our world changed.

The book includes a large cast of people. We will see Jesus as He walked on earth. I have taken some liberty with Bible stories as I've tried to imagine being there. We will see Pharisees and sinners, Old Testament characters, and everyday people like you and me. Some names have been changed and details altered slightly to protect identities, but I have received permission to share when possible.

The stories, which will take you on a journey of discovery, are woven together as a tapestry. You may see yourself on some pages, and those you know on others.

As you read I pray you will catch the rhythm of the Father's heart beating for you and people He brings to mind. This book is not intended to be merely read, but experienced. I have chosen small chapters to help you do that. There are questions to **Pause & Ponder**. Don't feel pressured! Some questions you may think about briefly and go on. If you struggle in an area, though, or feel a little nudge of the Holy Spirit, I encourage you to take the time to dig deeper. Ask the Lord to help you with the answers and experience His revelation in a fresh new way. There are **Journaling Tips** in the back to assist you. Work through the book by yourself or with a friend, or small group. Wrestle, discuss, contemplate, and pray. Some things may be no struggle for you, but may be helpful to others in your life.

The Lord has much to share with you.

It's the habits…
daily choices…
and attitudes of the heart TODAY
that determine our destiny and our freedom.
TODAY if you hear His voice, do not harden your heart.
Joy awaits!

— Marilyn Hume

❧ 1 ❧

ℐ Voice Crying

"Boo!"

"Go home!"

"Hmmph! I don't want to listen to that!" Jeers spread like wildfire through the crowd at the waterfront as some young men turned from singing catchy tunes to declaring that Jesus died for the sins of those gathered. There was no fire and brimstone in their message, just a sincere concern for the people's spiritual state. Amidst the merchants and carnival atmosphere at the annual city festival, and shortly after scandals had emerged about some internationally-known Christian personalities, the street preachers were not well received.

Frankly, I was shocked and fearful of the crowd's response. I had never felt this kind of tension or rejection of the gospel before. It seemed the wind had changed and a new course was firmly set.

As I stood on the outer perimeter of the crowd to see what would happen next, I asked the unkempt, apparently homeless man with bloodshot eyes, and breath reeking of alcohol next to me what he thought about what was being said. At first he said he couldn't understand or believe in a God who allowed bad things to happen to people.

This was a familiar argument, "Let's blame God for all the evil in the world; then I'm not responsible for rejecting Him."

But the man continued, as he choked on the words, "Why did God allow my wife and son to die in the fire when our house burned down?" Then he told about his time in Vietnam. He shuddered as though trying to wipe away the painful memories. "We did awful things..." and he described in horrible detail the destruction of innocent women and children.

I was surprised he shared these things with a total stranger. His inhibitions must have been weakened by his drunken state.

Then he cried as he bitterly spit out the words, "My dad used to beat me on my back with barbed wire. I have the scars to prove it!"

It was no wonder he had difficulty believing in a good God, or that he tried to drown his sorrows in a bottle. But try as he might, they would never fit inside. He had come home physically from Vietnam, but this man was still a prisoner of war.

Although I had never been in Vietnam, I could understand some of what he felt. I shared some of my story with him and how I gained freedom from some of my own inner prisons. Total strangers a few moments before, we were now drawn together by the memory of our painful wounds.

Our backwoods, small towns, and cities are filled with similar people — prisoners of war, missing in action, whether in our homes, on our streets, in board rooms or influential places, behind plows, flipping burgers, or in our churches:

- People who long for relationship, yet hide behind impenetrable walls, or use anger, criticism and judgments as a weapon of self-protection in a world where they have learned it's not safe to trust.
- People bound by addictions that dull their accusing voices and internal pain, who desperately long to be free.
- People created to gaze upon the beauty of the Lord and declare what they see upon the earth, now filled with shame and plagued with images that won't go away.
- People who cry out for understanding as David once did:

   If an enemy were insulting me, I could endure it; if a foe were raising himself against me, I could hide from him. But it is you, a man like myself, my companion, my close friend, with whom I once enjoyed sweet fellowship as we walked with the throng at the house of God. — Psalm 55:12-14 NIV

- People sidelined with lesser pursuits and mind-numbing activities to quiet the nagging question, "Is this all there is?"

• People like you and me.

But somewhere deep inside a cry is emerging. The voice of our Creator, seemingly long silent, is wooing us to come home, to be free, to discover who God created us to be. It is time!

A MAN CALLED JOHN

After four hundred years of silence except for the conquering hoof beats and marching feet of foreign armies, God stepped into time. He spoke once again to a people captive in their own homeland through a man promised by the prophet Malachi who would "*restore the hearts of the fathers to their children and the hearts of the children to their fathers* (Malachi 4:6)."

People from miles around, young and old, rich and poor, government officials, religious leaders, and even dreaded Roman soldiers, gathered together by the Jordan River.[1] For a brief moment in time who or what they were was temporarily suspended, as John's words penetrated past their reasoning minds. Untold numbers confessed their sins and were baptized by him in the river.

But what attracted them? It obviously was not his charming, winsome ways. In fact, his words at times seemed downright rude.

"You brood of vipers, who warned you to flee from the wrath to come?" his voice echoed through the group of Pharisees and Sadducees coming for baptism, "Bear fruit in keeping with repentance!"

How could this man reconcile the generations?

If he were to stand on the doorsteps of our churches today you may hear shouted, "Do those things that prove you have turned to God and have changed the way you think and act!"[2]

Some would be offended, even as they were back then. Many would dismiss him as a crazed man, or whisper words of judgment, "Where's the love? Where's the grace?"

But others would hear in his voice the pleading of heaven, and the tearful cries of millions of captives estranged from God and one another, who are waiting for just such a people to arise in the earth—

passionate lovers who demonstrate the very life and substance of a supernatural, world-changing God. A people who will be free from their own prisons, then see the treasure beyond the rags and bondage of others, seek them out and joyfully welcome them home.

Creation groans…

Hearts long…

When will they appear?

PAUSE & PONDER…

Take a few moments to answer the following questions. See introduction for further instructions.

1. Can you identify with any of the people described as prisoners of war? What about people you know?

2. What do you think "a people who exhibit the very life and substance of a supernatural, world-changing God" are like? Are you that type of person?

---

[1] Matthew 3:1-10

[2] Matthew 3:8 GW

❧ 2 ❧
Who is This Man?

One day another man emerged from the wilderness. There was nothing about His appearance that would cause people to be attracted to Him. But there was a power, a presence about Him that defied indifference. Those who drew near were either compelled to come closer or repelled by an unseen clash in the spirit realm.

Those compelled followed Him to Nazareth, His home town, in the hills of the Galilean region.

They pondered. "No man speaks like this man. No one does the things He does!"

"Who is He?"

Oh, many were acquainted with Jesus, the man, the son of Joseph. But they couldn't explain His power and authority. This son of the carpenter had the bearing of a king, yet without pretense.

"Who *is* He?"

THE SPIRIT OF THE LORD IS ON ME

As was His habit, He entered the Synagogue on the Sabbath Day. Some were puzzled by why people jostled one another to get into the seats around Him. They had not heard the news of His recent preaching in the surrounding areas. Some only knew Him as Jesus, the young man who frequently sat among them since childhood. But today a hush descended on all as He stood up to read. When the scroll of the book of Isaiah was placed in His hands by the attendant, He slowly unrolled one side and re-rolled the other, until He came to the place where it was written:

The Spirit of the Lord is on me, because He has anointed Me to preach good news to the poor. He has sent Me to proclaim freedom for the prisoners and recovery of sight for the blind, to release the oppressed, to proclaim the year of the Lord's favor.
—Isaiah 61:1,2 NIV

The words were familiar to any who frequented the synagogue, but something was different. Hearts were gripped, emotions stirred as these words on *this* day penetrated as never before.

The Man closed the book, gave it back to the attendant and sat down, but the people were stunned, their eyes fixed on Him.[1] Catching their gaze He said, *"Today this scripture has been fulfilled in your hearing."* (See Luke 4.)

If you listened closely you could hear faint little gasps, as hearts leaped unexpectedly, and minds tried to grasp, "What does He mean?"

Those acquainted with the Law believed *'...the year of the Lord's favor"* was when all Israel would be set free. Jubilee, the year of release, symbolized this freedom. The commandments flashed in microseconds through their minds. For six years they were supposed to till the land, plant, and harvest, but in the seventh, or Sabbath year, they were to let the land rest, trust God to provide, and free their servants.

Then in the fiftieth year, or after seven Sabbath years... Thoughts slowed and foreheads wrinkled, "Oh, what was different that year?" A few fingers counted off the recalled instructions one by one. "Oh yeah, that's right, they were to again let the land rest, and on the Day of Atonement they were to:

- Blow a trumpet and declare a year of Jubilee
- Proclaim liberty to all who were enslaved
- Buy back those taken captive to other nations
- Return to the land received through inheritance
- Gather again in families
- Cancel all debts, and restore everything to its rightful owner." (See Leviticus 25.)

Justice was restored as all the inequities of the past were settled, and everyone got a fresh start.

But under Roman rule there was no Jubilee. No freedom. No justice or cancellation of debts. They were prisoners of war, captives in their own nation. Where was their promised Messiah—the one who would deliver them from Roman rule? It seemed as though God had turned His back on them for so long.

Anger welled up in the hearts of some now.

But, honestly, it wasn't just Roman rule; Jubilee had not been celebrated for centuries! Anger gave way to morbid hopelessness at the thought.

Questions like butting rams collided in the heads of those gathered. "What could He mean?"

This man...The unmistakable look of love in His eyes...His words...

"Today this scripture is fulfilled in your ears."

Hope, refusing to be fettered, sparked within them.

A fresh start. Could it be? The faint whisper of unutterable truth welled up like a bubbling spring deep within, "JUBILEE IS HERE!?

JUBILEE IS HERE.

What a profound statement! Even though the people were amazed at the words of Jesus and their hearts burned within them, they could not fully comprehend what this Man was saying. Neither can we. This was not a series of dates on the calendar comprising one year, but a line in the sand, a fixed boundary, an altering of destinies. His words were like the blast of a trumpet declaring the end of everything that had gone on before and activating a new transformational kingdom in the world.

The King has come to bring justice, settle accounts, and establish permanent residence. He's approachable, and in a good mood.

Nothing would ever be the same again. Jubilee, always God's heart for His people, was now available to all who, as much loved children of their Father, would dare believe and receive--not just every fifty years but an ongoing reality of this new kingdom:

- All the accumulated debts and inequities of the past cancelled, and justice reestablished.

- Prisoners of war set free, and missing in action brought home again.
- Sickness and disease healed.
- Nagging voices that accuse, threaten, and demand performance of ourselves and others silenced.
- Relationships with God, family, friends, and people groups restored.
- Lost inheritances, and unfulfilled destinies regained.
- Hope and sense of safety renewed.
- Lives permeated with rest and filled with joy.
- Surrounding chaos invaded with peace flowing from within us.[2]

One of the profound truths that Jesus came to bring is that if we want to walk in Jubilee and have our own debts cancelled, there are debts we must cancel.

To experience freedom we must set our own captives free.

You may say, "What captives do I have?"

But on closer look we see we all have them—some more obvious than others, but still there. We keep people locked in "boxes" of our own judgments of who we think they are. We look on outward appearances and see through the grid of our own wounding. The Bible is very clear:

> *Do not judge so that you will not be judged. For in the way you judge, you will be judged; and by your standard of measure, it will be measured to you.* —Matthew 7:1-2

When we hold others captive in the prisons of our judgments, we too are held captive.

Also, we can easily miss out on wonderful resources of wisdom, understanding, and compassion by closing our hearts and minds to those we judge by our own standard of measurement.

Ultimately, the people in the synagogue drove Jesus out of town because they could not get past their own judgments.

A pastor came to visit our family one day in the old farmhouse on the camp property where we lived and worked. He looked around, liked what he saw, and said, "Now I know that you are quality people."

I suppose he meant it as a compliment, but I couldn't help but wonder, "Who did you think we were before you entered our home? By what standard were you measuring us?"

I love what Paul said:

> *... we don't evaluate people by what they have or how they look. We looked at the Messiah that way once and got it all wrong, as you know. We certainly don't look at Him that way anymore.*
> —2 Corinthians 5:16 *The Message*

God uses a much different measuring system than our own:

GOD'S MEASURE

THE MEASURE OF CHARACTER
Who I am when no one is looking
... God sees not as man sees, for man looks at the outward appearance, but the LORD looks at the heart. —1 Samuel 16:7

THE MEASURE OF MATURITY
How I respond to opposition
...Consider it pure joy, My brothers, whenever you face trials of many kinds, because you know that the testing of your faith develops perseverance. Perseverance must finish its work so that you may be mature and complete, not lacking anything. —James 1:2-4

THE MEASURE OF GREATNESS
My ability to joyfully serve others
The greatest among you shall be your servant. —Matthew 23:11

THE MEASURE OF SUCCESS
The degree to which I hear the word of God and obey it
This book of the law shall not depart from your mouth, but you shall meditate on it day and night, so that you may be careful to do according to all that is written in it; for then you will make your way prosperous, and then you will have success. —Joshua 1:8

THE MEASURE OF RELATIONSHIP WITH GOD
My love for others
The one who does not love does not know God, for God is love." —1 John 4:8

Yes, we have our boxes of judgments. But they say more about us than the ones we hold captive.

PAUSE & PONDER…

1. Imagine yourself seeing Jesus for the first time, experiencing His words and presence. Would you have felt compelled or repelled? Why?

2. Have you ever misjudged someone?

   When you laid aside your judgments, how did that person enrich your life?

3. What do you think Jubilee would look like for you in these areas? Ask the Lord to help you see through His eyes:

   - Rest
   - Debts cancelled
   - Justice reestablished
   - Captives set free
   - Things lost restored
   - Families reunited and healed
   - Recovery of sight to the blind

---

[1] A regular schedule was usually followed in the synagogue, so this was probably the assigned reading. The teacher of the day would sit down to teach, so that could also explain why all eyes were still upon Jesus.

[2] As the kingdom of God is preached with demonstration of the Spirit and of power (1 Corinthians 2:4) and invades the kingdoms of this earth, we will experience more of the reality of Jubilee.

❧ 3 ❧
The Measure of Love

To some who were confident of their own righteousness and looked down on everybody else, Jesus told this parable:

"Two men went up to the temple to pray, one a Pharisee and the other a tax collector. The Pharisee stood up and prayed about himself: 'God, I thank you that I am not like other men — robbers, evildoers, adulterers — or even like this tax collector. I fast twice a week and give a tenth of all I get.' But the tax collector stood at a distance. He would not even look up to heaven, but beat his breast and said, 'God, have mercy on me, a sinner.'

"I tell you that this man, rather than the other, went home justified before God. For everyone who exalts himself will be humbled, and he who humbles himself will be exalted."

– Luke 18:9-14 NIV

I confess that too often I have found myself in the Pharisee's robes of self-righteousness rather than in the sinner's sackcloth of repentance.

Both men in the parable were at the same place at the same time. One found God, one did not. One was a sinner by man's standards, one was not. But, the tax collector went home forgiven that day, while the Pharisee did not. He missed his day of visitation.

I don't suppose the Pharisee started out that way. He probably began as a sincere young man who wanted to serve God, but he lived in a system that valued performance more than relationship, judgments more than grace. In fact, the very name Pharisee meant to be separate from others. When you take on a name, soon the name begins to define your character. If that name is counter to the nature of God, you can become someone other than who God intended you to be.

The Pharisee saw the Law as a book of rules instead of a letter of love. He knew a lot of what the scrolls said about the God whose name was too holy to speak, but he arbitrarily chose to forget that God is no respecter of persons, that He is gracious and compassionate, and He loves a broken and contrite heart.

Somewhere along the road the Pharisee lost love.

WHAT IS LOVE?

If love is the measure of whether or not we truly have relationship with God, what is it? An ooshy-gooshy feeling that overwhelms you, or a choice devoid of emotion? Is it an act of kindness, or warm sentimentality?

First Corinthians 13:4-8 NIV says:

> *Love is patient, love is kind. It does not envy, it does not boast, it is not proud. It is not rude, it is not self-seeking, it is not easily angered, it keeps no record of wrongs. Love does not delight in evil but rejoices with the truth. It always protects, always trusts, always hopes, always perseveres. Love never fails….*

Just to hear about love lifts my spirits, soothes my soul. Oh, love is so grand, so splendid, so lofty…so impossible!

I think I've always wanted to love. I remember Sabrina, the young girl in my grade school who was always alone and rarely spoke. Her straight black hair, cut in an even line from jaw to jaw, and her hooked nose added to the mystery of this little one whose mother walked her to school every day. The mother, whose gray hair was always tied down with a scarf, looked to childish minds like she stepped right out of the pages of a fairy tale. Was her vehicle a broomstick?

Sabrina became the object of whispers and open ridicule, as children are prone to do in the absence of knowledge. It was rumored that her father was in prison. But, honestly, I never got close enough to find out. Oh, I was never mean to her. I couldn't do that. In fact, I would sometimes daydream about turning this little ugly duckling into a swan, this uncomely Cinderella into a princess. But they were only daydreams. The truth was, I wanted to be kind, but I didn't want to be identified with her. After all, what would other kids think of me?

I didn't take the time to love.

But I did try with Herman Yoder. Yes, he really did live on the other side of the tracks in a little old shack. My father, a letter carrier, delivered mail to his home but knew little about the old man with spindly legs, a round belly, and very few teeth in his bald head. Herman would come and sit alone on the back pew of our church from time to time when I was young. Now when I say back pew, I don't mean the last in a series. I mean a pew against the back wall several feet from any others.

When I was a teenager I decided to not let his visits go unnoticed, so I would take a deep breath, put on my best smile, amble over to Herman, and engage him in small talk, "How ya doin'? Good to have ya here..."

When I went away to college some of the other youth in the church began to show love to old Herman. One year they took a collection and bought him a blanket for Christmas. The small acts of kindness were working their way into his heart.

One day at the end of a service Herman left his back pew and walked the long distance to the front of the church, knelt, and gave his heart to the Lord. I wish I could have been there to see it. Not long after that Herman died.

We have no idea the change we can make in someone's life by just taking the time to say, "Hello," or speak a kind word of encouragement—to love when others would turn away.

We have, however, seen those who felt judged, unloved, ridiculed and uncared for walk into schools or businesses and open gunfire on guilty and innocent alike, as if this would somehow solve all the hurt and rejection they had experienced. They picked up weapons of war to fight free from their own prisons within.

Gary Chapman in his classic book, *The Five Love Languages,*[1] points out five different ways we receive love:

- Words of affirmation
- Acts of Kindness
- Quality Time
- Physical Touch
- Giving of Gifts

It's important to learn to love others the way they best receive it, but love must be more than a theory or a formula to be followed. Otherwise it can be manipulation, devoid of life-giving power. Love must flow from the heart. The full expression of God's love is found in Jesus Christ.

HE IS OUR EXAMPLE OF HOW TO LOVE

He gave **gifts** of healing to multitudes in need.

In the cover of night, He spent **quality time** with Nicodemus, a religious ruler seeking truth who was afraid to be seen with Jesus in the light of day.

Jesus easily identified with the outcasts of society. He spoke the truth in love to a woman caught in adultery, and **words of affirmation** to a prostitute who washed His feet with her tears and dried them with her hair.

He gave up lunch to stand beside a well in the heat of the day to talk with a Samaritan woman who had been married five times, and was now living with another man. I don't know what His Father told Him beforehand, maybe it was just a simple nudge, "Don't go with the guys to get food, stay here and wait. There's someone I want you to meet." Food was unimportant that day. Jesus found loving others as He saw His Father doing a more satisfying feast.

Lepers by law went through the streets crying, "Unclean, unclean..." drawing unwanted attention to themselves. Every day they were faced with the horror of their disease as it ravaged their flesh and emitted an unbearable stench. Yet Jesus reached out and **touched** them, restoring their dignity.

He showed **kindness** to Zaccheus, a little man in a tree, a dreaded tax collector, hated by other men. But Jesus chose to spend time with him—a kindness that led Zaccheus to repentance.

Love is not easily angered; however, His love propelled Him to drive the moneychangers out of the temple so the poor and needy could come and receive what God desperately wanted to give them.

Jesus was a friend to sinners, unlike the Pharisee. He lived the language of love everyday as He went about setting people free from those things that held them captive.

How did He stay filled with love?

He received it. He spent time with His Father, hearing His words of affirmation, listening to His heart until they beat as one.

He did not look to men for approval, nor was He crushed when rejection and ridicule came His way. He lived as a free man, Jubilee within, as He walked among those in captivity.

He kept His gaze fixed on the eyes of His Father. As a result, His identity was secure—he knew who He was and where He was going, and He loved as He was loved.

He said that we are to love others too, but many times our judgments get in the way.

It is Time

PAUSE & PONDER...

1. How would your family describe your relationship with God? Your friends or co-workers? Other drivers on the freeway?

2. Have you ever been part of a broken religious system that valued performance over relationship, as exhibited in the story of the Pharisee and the tax collector?

3. How did you feel about God in that system? Yourself? Others? How did your view of God change? Or how is it changing today?

---

[1] Gary Chapman, *The Five Love Languages*, (Moody Publishers, 1992)

☞ 4 ☜
Judgments Kill

"Hi, honey, glad you made it home safely. Could you ask Johnny something for me?" We—my children, my son's friend and I—just returned from visiting my parents in Idaho when I got the phone call. I quickly recognized my mother's voice as she went on to explain what had happened. Some friends of my sister who lived in California were passing through town and wanted to see my parents. Two or three of my aunts and uncles were already at their house, so Mom invited these friends to come join them for dinner. Mom, wanting to make a good impression, quickly scurried about fixing a nice meal.

After a pleasant time visiting, the friends left.

As my relatives were still sitting at the table chatting, Mom happened to glance up and see the chandelier in the living room, which was in full sight of everyone at the dining room table. She was horrified by what she saw, and gasped as her mouth flew open. Eyes around the table followed hers, and sounds of surprise and laughter erupted. Hanging from the chandelier was a pair of my mother's underpants!

Mom's nice day turned into one of embarrassment and anxiety, "Did the friends see? How long have they been there?" When she thought we'd finally returned home she gave us a call and asked, "Does Johnny know anything about it?"

I found out he did. He and his friend discovered them between the cushions of the couch where Mom frequently folded clothes, and just gave them a toss. Oops!

Why do we worry about what others think? Maybe it is because people can be quite cruel in their judgments.

When I was young we usually spent a couple weeks each summer at a beautiful lake in a resort town, where we often attended a little church on Sunday mornings. One day a visiting missionary was the guest speaker. I still remember and cringe at the feeling I had that day when this man pounded on the pulpit and yelled with a loud angry voice, "There's only one way for a woman to wear her hair! UNCUT!"

Knowing I was guilty, I slithered down into the pew, wishing I could make my hair appear longer than it was.

No one came to Jesus THAT day.

Sometimes, when we attended the church's camp meetings a few of our friends wore hairpieces because they didn't want to feel the condemnation of others.

When judgments are prevalent, it is very easy to put on a mask. The problem is, after a while we have no truth in relationships because everyone is trying to be someone else so they won't get judged!

While on vacation my husband and I stopped at a hot springs to soak in the soothing mineral water. A man swam over to us and immediately asked if we were Christians.

"Yes," we said with a smile.

Then he announced the church he attended, which I knew by their advertisements centered more on what they didn't believe than on the grace of Christ. Next he asked our view on a particular point of theology that has caused division for years. By the way he asked the question it appeared he wanted to debate the issue. I answered him in support of both views, because each has validity, but graciously let him know I didn't want to get drawn into a dispute.

It was obvious my answer didn't meet his approval, and he wandered away. We could have had rich fellowship together as believers, but he seemed only interested in proving his point. Sometimes I want to retort, "Why do you strain over the interpretation of a few scriptures, and miss the most important one to love the Lord with all your heart, soul, mind, and strength, and your neighbor as yourself?" (See Matthew 22:37-39.) It's amazing how many things we find to divide us:

- Political and world views, isms and ideologies
- Doctrines and biblical interpretation
- Morality and sin
- Style, freedom, size and place of worship
- Habits, personal preference, attire, and appearance
- Race, gender, and past history
- Source of gifts or deeds — God, the devil, or the flesh
- And much more.

The arguments can be quite confusing and depressing. God has called us to build HIS kingdom. Instead we've created whole movements based on our biases and judgments.

I have often maintained that the greatest enemy of the gospel is not any other religion, sin, or ideology of men; the gospel's greatest enemies are Christians who:

- Say one thing and do another
- Claim to have the love of Christ, but exhibit anger, hatred and bitterness toward other believers and the world
- Preach the power of the gospel, but live powerless lives.

Like wells without water in a desert place, we leave the world feeling hopeless and disillusioned. That hopelessness and disillusionment can easily give way to anger in a world desperate for a drink.

Mahatma Gandhi, when asked about the message of Jesus Christ, replied:

"It is better to allow our lives to speak for us than our words…It would be poor comfort to the world, if it had to depend upon a historical God who died two thousand years ago. Do not then preach the God of history but show Him as He lives today through you…"[1]

Jesus did tell us to preach, but our lives must match our message. James 3:8 tells us that *"no one can tame the tongue; it is a restless evil and full of deadly poison."* Sometimes the words don't even come out of our mouths. Jesus frequently called people into account for their judgmental thoughts. Why? Such thoughts create an atmosphere where relationships are destroyed, faith cannot grow, and doors to demonic influence are opened.

VIOLINS AND PENNIES

At some point we have all judged or been judged by others. Hanging over the desk in my office is a copy of "The Old Violin," an oil painting I saw at the National Gallery of Art in Washington DC. The original was so life-like I had to get up very close to see that it was, in fact, a painting. It reminded me of a poem I memorized in my eighth grade English Literature class that continually calls me to lay aside my own judgments.

The poem, "The Touch of the Master's Hand," by Myra Brooks Welch, tells about an old violin that is on the auction block at a very cheap price until a man comes forward and shows its true beauty and worth as he cleans, adjusts, and plays a beautiful melody on it. Mrs. Welch likens the old violin to "many a man with life out of tune, and battered and scarred with sin," who is "auctioned cheap to the thoughtless crowd, much like the old violin." She goes on to say:

> "But the Master comes, and the foolish crowd
> Never can quite understand
> The worth of a soul and the change that's wrought
> By the touch of the Master's hand."[3]

I've experienced His touch.

My life as I knew it was on the verge of shattering, and I felt worthless, insignificant, and unloved. Even the breathtaking view of the beautiful valley with its lush green trees and velvety hillsides framed by the shimmering water below could not console me. I had come to this favorite spot to get away and talk to God, but it seemed difficult to even reach Him.

Glancing down the dirt trail, I saw a grimy old penny lying in the dust. Pennies were of little value to some of those closest to me, who frequently discarded them as an irritation.

"God," I cried out, "I feel worthless just like that penny!"

Then, ever so softly, not audibly, but deep in my spirit, I heard Jesus speak, "Marilyn, whose face is on that penny?"

"Well, Abraham Lincoln, of course."

"Would he think it was worthless? After all, his image is imprinted on it. Not only that, he died for his country."

Feeling mildly corrected I responded, "You're right, Lord, I doubt he would think it was worthless."

The Lord continued, "Don't you know that you're of far greater value to me, for in every cell and fiber of your being you are stamped with the very image of God. Not only that, I gave My life for you. You are priceless to Me. Don't ever call yourself worthless."

The tender yet powerful weight of His words broke through the bonds of my pain.

"Oh, Lord, I'm sorry! Please forgive me!"

A moment of despair was transformed into a precious encounter with the Living God. My circumstances didn't immediately change, but my view of them did. Now when I see pennies lying on the ground, whether bright and shiny, or dirty and misshapen, on carpet, or in the gutter, I pick them up. They are a simple, constant reminder to never judge or regard anyone as worthless.

Is it always easy? No.

One day I drove down the road near our home and saw a man trying to walk a straight line under a policeman's watchful gaze. He failed miserably. My first thoughts were, "He's just an old drunk!" But as I got closer I realized he was my neighbor, the husband of a sweet woman, a father, grandfather, and friend to many. He was caught in the clutches of a miserable addiction and desperately needed to experience the love of God. My neighbor became an object of prayer when God opened my eyes to his need.

Each person is imprinted with the image of God, no matter how tarnished or hidden. God is calling us to be treasure hunters who lay aside the bitter water of our judgments and condemnation, uncover the beauty of who God created them to be, and allow to flow through us living water that refreshes and heals.

"…Jesus stood and cried out, saying,
"If anyone is thirsty, let him come to Me and drink." –John 7:37

PAUSE & PONDER…

1. Have you put on any masks to keep from being judged?

2. Do others feel they have to wear masks with you to get your approval?

   If so, ask the Lord to show you how you can extend acceptance and love to them.

3. Have you ever felt like a worthless penny?

4. Pray "Lord, show me how much You love me. Open my eyes to see the treasure I am to You." Now sit quietly and listen, with your mind focused on the Lord. Write down what comes into your thoughts.

---

[1] Mahatma Gandhi, *All Men Are Brothers: Autobiographical Reflections*, Krishna Kripalani, Contributor (Continuum International Publishing Group, 1980), 55

[2] William Michael Harnett, "The Old Violin," 1886

[3] Myra Brooks Welch, "The Touch of the Master's Hand,"1926, Public Domain

❧ 5 ❧
Why Do We Judge?

Kids learn to be critical quite early, and their teasing can be merciless. When I was in sixth grade our family moved to a new area, and I had to change schools mid-year. Being new I faced expectations I couldn't attain. Someone heard I was a fast runner but I turned out to be just average. Another gal was afraid I would steal her boyfriend. I felt like others were reading a script of who I was according to their expectations but failed to let me in on the story.

So, when I heard some boys teasing a girl, "Wow, you have big feet!" and saw her wither under their scathing jibes, I determined I would never wear shoes THAT big. As a result I wore shoes that were too tight for many years. My damaged feet are a constant reminder of my foolishness! (For the record, my shoe size IS bigger than hers now, and I've lived to tell about it!)

Those seemingly insignificant events increased my fear of the judgments of others.

Let's take a look at a few reasons why we are critical and judgmental:

Judging can be a **learned habit**. Some of us grew up in homes where we shared a lot with one another, but there is a line between the simple communication of information, gossip, and critical judgments. What really needs to be shared? Are we honoring others with our words in casual conversation?

It can also be **learned prejudice** — a problem in every country and culture. The issues may change, but prejudice remains.

I didn't know any African-Americans until I was in junior high, when I met a nice young man who attended our school. Before then I was quite ignorant about blacks because there were very few in my home town. They looked different, yet similar at the same time. In my childish innocence I wondered if inside the dark skin they were like me, similar to the way I wondered at an early age if doctors did tests on babies to determine if they were boys or girls. I had only seen diapers, not what was underneath them!

I honestly didn't think I had any prejudice toward blacks until my daughter dated a handsome African-American. I tried to dismiss it as concern that their potential children could face prejudice, but finally had to admit there was some in me. Why, I don't know. It may have been a reaction to a married black man I worked with who tried to pick up on me. It's unfair to judge an entire race or people group by the actions of one or even a few persons. When I realized my prejudice, I repented and asked God to forgive me.

Later, when I took part in a city-wide prayer meeting in a predominantly black area of the city where I live, one of the leaders turned to me on the platform and asked if I had something to share. At first I didn't think so, but then felt impressed that I needed to ask the blacks in attendance to forgive my prejudice. What amazed me was how many came up after the meeting and asked me to forgive them. They said if their son or daughter had brought home someone white they would have been prejudiced too!

Another reason we judge is **fear. We want to be safe.** If we've been wounded in the past, we create systems to avoid being re-injured. One of the ways we do that is to thoroughly investigate people, perceive their motives (real or imagined), and know their faults so we can watch out for any potential land mines in our relationship with them.

Similarly, if we have allowed bitterness to enter, we look for those who are just like the one who wounded us or someone we love, and become self-appointed judges **to keep the world safe.** We may have a strong sense of justice, and feel it is our job to right all the wrongs in society.

Sometimes it's **self-justification.** If we have difficulty forgiving ourselves or have received judgments, we may subconsciously feel the need to prove we are better than others. It's as though we are constantly being weighed on an imaginary scale and found wanting. So we try to even up the scales by finding the shortcomings in others. We have not learned to receive God's grace.

Why? It's because we often have a **wrong view of God**. We think we have to earn His favor and it's not easy! When my children were learning to walk I didn't get mad at them when they fell down. Instead I cheered them on every time they took a few steps, and then joyfully helped them up when they stumbled and encouraged them to try again. I am an imperfect parent, but God is our perfect Father who responds with much more love and care. He's always good, even when we fail. He wants us to have that same heart toward ourselves and others.

Judgments can also stem from **unmet expectations**. In his book *The Shack*, William P. Young writes:

[Holy Spirit speaking] "I know you and everything about you. Why would I have an expectation other than what I already know? ...I have no expectations, you never disappoint me...What I do have is a constant and living expectancy in our relationship, and I give you an ability to respond to any situation and circumstance in which you find yourself. To the degree that you resort to expectations and responsibilities, to that degree you neither know me nor trust me."[1]

We then in turn put these expectations on others. Jesus said in John 15:9, *"Just as the Father has loved me, I have also loved you; abide in My love."* Abide means to stay in a given place, state, relation or expectancy.[2] As we abide in God's presence, and learn to live in a sense of expectancy with Him, it is easier to let go of our unfulfilled expectations of others.

There's also the **downside of spiritual gifts**. For instance, someone gifted with mercy may be critical of others who are not merciful according to their standard. Or someone with the gift of helps or giving may condemn those who don't see and respond to needs in the same way.

A teacher may perceive a better way. While writing this book I have been painfully aware of how I can negatively affect my own children. I want the best for them, and when I see there's a way life could go easier, I want to share. But coming from Mom, it feels critical and judgmental. But I am committed to change the way I communicate with the Lord's help!

Someone with a gift of discernment may use his gift to build walls instead of bridges. This gift is the ability to discern between right and wrong, truth and error, divine, human, or demonic spirits, and godly or carnal motives.

Wall builders react with fear or anger and warn others, "Do you see that?! You better stay away from him!"

Bridge builders, filled with compassion and peace, respond first to God, "Yes, Lord, I see that. How do You want me to lay down my life as a bridge over which You can bring healing and restoration to him?"

Sometimes it is simply **lack of knowledge** — we really don't know any better.

When I was young I spent a lot of time at a girlfriend's house playing dolls and horses. We had great times together, but because Jody was a couple of years older, we eventually grew apart as she entered junior high. One Saturday I was playing at the local grade school when I saw Jody and a boy go into a stairwell. Curious, I went to see what they were doing. Can you believe it? They were hugging and kissing!

Okay, I should have left. But I didn't. I kept watching, until Jody happened to glance up and see me. I quickly ran away, but later she found and tackled me, knocking me to the ground. Then she sat straddle legged on my tummy, and pummeled me with her flailing hands. At the same time she screamed, "You always told me I would go to hell if I didn't give my heart to Jesus!"

I was stunned and mortified (besides a little bruised!). I didn't remember telling her that, but knew she wouldn't make it up. In Sunday School I heard stories about people who died before giving their hearts to Jesus, and out of concern for my friend I must have tried to save her from the flames of hell. But to my friend, I just sounded critical and judgmental.

Many years later I ran into her at a high school reunion. After a little initial awkwardness I asked her to forgive me for how I had offended her. "Jesus really loves you, and I'm sorry I didn't represent Him well to you."

Yes, there is the reality of future judgment, but there is a vast difference between conviction and condemnation. I had condemned her, but the Bible is clear, "… *the kindness of God leads us to repentance*" (Romans 2:4).

Although, God can use that incident to bring her to Him, it would have been better to love her into the kingdom than to point out her sins and shortcomings! I have prayed God would send someone else to witness to her in a more loving way.

WE CAN BECOME UNOFFENDABLE

King Solomon, the author of Ecclesiastes, understood the prevalence of our judgments:

> *Indeed, there is not a righteous man on earth who continually does good and who never sins. Also, do not take seriously all words which are spoken, so that you will not hear your servant cursing you. For you also have realized that you likewise have many times cursed others.* — Ecclesiastes 7:20-22

That's why it's important to treat others the way we would like to be treated. We don't make excuses for ourselves when we are accused of offending others, no matter how irrational or petty the alleged offense may be. We honor the other person's opinion and do what we can to bring peace.

Conversely, we try to mature to the point where we don't get offended by everything. We expect the best of people's motives and intentions, instead of suspect them.

Some good questions to ask ourselves are:

Is this a loving thing to think or say?
- Am I getting offended when someone may simply not have the ability to express himself better or act differently?

- What is intentional, what is lack of skill?
- Is this something that really needs to be confronted or covered with God's grace? Wayne Cordeiro says, "Loving people means that we remain committed to God's very best for their lives. If God's best means overlooking a fault or indiscretion, than we overlook it. If God's best is to confront, then we will confront in love."[3]

The answers to these questions require a new depth of intimacy with the Lord. We must learn to hear His heart for others.

Jesus did not allow some people to push Him off a cliff, because He knew it wasn't His day to die. But He didn't get angry or confront them. He just calmly and peacefully walked through the midst of them (Luke 4:28-30).

It's important to remember that we are not here to live a life of comfort. We are here to expand the kingdom of God, and love is the atmosphere, the life-giving air, in His kingdom. Jesus said we are to love our enemies, do good to those who hate us, bless those who curse us, give to everyone who asks, lend without expecting repayment, and be merciful as He is merciful (see Luke 7:27-37). He called us to a whole new level of righteousness, and modeled it for us. He's also given us His Holy Spirit to empower us to live the same way. Yes, Jesus acknowledges and heals our hurts, but He also wants us to get hurt less often. Love "...*is not irritable or touchy. It does not hold grudges and will hardly even notice when others do it wrong*" (1 Corinthians 13:5 TLB).

God really loves people, and He is passionate about YOU! That knowledge enables us to more easily love others and let go of offenses. But no one ever said loving is easy.

❧ ◆ ❧

PAUSE & PONDER…

1. Explore the following list of judgmental reasons, which ones do you struggle with the most? Underline or circle the ones you intend to work on:

   • Learned habit
   • Learned prejudice
   • Fear: we want to be safe
   • We want to keep the world safe
   • Self-justification
   • Wrong view of God
   • Unmet expectations
   • Down-side of spiritual gifts
   • Lack of knowledge

2. Ask the Lord to show you:

   a. The root cause of that struggle. Sit quietly until He brings revelation. It may come in the form of a word, a picture, or a scene from your past.

   b. Any lies associated with that root, such as, "I will never be good enough," or "No one will ever really love me."

   c. What is the truth?

3. How would life be different if you were healed of those judgments?

   Are you ready?

If so, pray:

> "Heavenly Father, heal my heart of judgmental attitudes. Help
> me erase the prejudices and habits that brought them about. I
> renounce the lie(s) I have believed that _____,
> and choose to embrace the truth that _____.
> Give me a new understanding of Your love and grace, and teach
> me to love like Jesus. Amen."

[1] William P. Young, *The Shack* (Windblown Media, 2007), 204-206
[2] James Strong, S.T.D., LL.D., *Strong's Exhaustive Concordance*, 1890, #3306
[3] Wayne Cordeiro, *Doing Church as a Team* (Regal Publishing, 2001, 2004), 158

Will You Love Him?

"Will you love him?"

I recognized the voice of the Lord deep in my spirit, but knew I could not give a pat answer. The events of the last few hours made that very clear. My husband Steve[1] was in the hospital for a minor operation. When I took him in the night before, he seemed quick to dismiss me as he jokingly flirted with the nurses. Although I sometimes felt insecure by his behavior, this time it was especially painful. A couple months earlier he revealed he'd been having an affair for several months. My whole world crashed down at the time. Simple things became difficult as every thought and action passed through a series of grids and second guessing, "Where is he? What is he doing? What's wrong with me? Why can't he love me? What can I do differently?" Eggshell walking became a tedious art in the awkwardness of each other's presence. He said the affair was over, but it takes time to reestablish trust. And this wasn't helping!

In a life-changing divine encounter at a youth camp when I was fifteen, I told the Lord He could do anything with my life that He wanted. I would go anywhere He sent me or be anything He wanted me to be.

But this? This was not at all what I expected! That was part of the problem. We married young with expectations we could not fulfill, and we both made lots of mistakes along the way.

After I left the hospital that night a sequence of events left me feeling more lonely, rejected, misunderstood, and humiliated. To anyone else they would have seemed nothing, in fact, somewhat humorous, but they further fueled my hopelessness and despair.

When I got the kids tucked in for the night I lay on my bed and contemplated what to do, as waves of anguish tormented my already fragile mind. Alone in the darkness the only thing that seemed to make any sense was the gun in the closet. Then all the hurt and pain would be over.

Done.

No more.

"But what about Jane?" My imaginations were interrupted at the thought.

A few months earlier my friend Jane sat in her car with the motor running in the closed garage because the pain in her life was more than she could bear. Her teenage daughter found her lifeless body, and it caused unbearable grief for her family and friends who loved her.

In spite of the rejection and hurt, I knew I couldn't do that to my children. So, I cried out to God and asked Him for strength to endure, and felt His loving arms bring comfort to my troubled soul. Then I fell into a deep sleep.

The next morning after getting the kids off to school I headed back to the hospital. It was in the car on the way when I heard, "Will you love him?"

"Can I love him? Will I choose to love him no matter what?" After a few moments of intense contemplation, with resolve in my spirit I said, "Yes, Lord, I will love him."

As I approached Steve's room, I heard him speaking. Wondering if someone was there, I lightened my steps and proceeded quietly. As I stood in the doorway in full view of Steve in his hospital bed, I saw he was talking on the telephone. The words, the tone of voice — it was unmistakable. He was talking to his "friend."

I stood there for a few moments wondering what to do as a mixture of anger, hurt, and disbelief filled my thoughts. Everything within me wanted to turn and run away. But the words echoed back, "Will you love him, Marilyn?"

I didn't think my commitment would be challenged so quickly! "Yes, Lord, I will love him," I painfully responded.

Eventually, Steve looked up, saw me standing in the doorway, and quickly changed the conversation. But, when confronted he could not deny the truth.

What now?
Deep breath.
One foot in front of the other.
I must love him through the imminent surgery.
Love today.

LOVE BEYOND REASON

There are times God calls us to love beyond natural reason. Abraham discovered something of the love and kindness of God when the Lord said his family would not be able to go into the land God promised them for another four hundred years. Why? The sin of the present inhabitants had not yet reached its full measure (Genesis 15:13-16).

It is difficult for us to comprehend that God would allow His own chosen people to suffer captivity in Egypt for so many years while the sins of the Amorites piled higher and higher, until God finally chose to act. Is God unjust in His actions? No. He eventually dealt righteous judgment on the unrepentant Amorites and revealed Himself as a loving Father, provider, and deliverer to the Israelites. "Whatever you need, I AM!"

Sometimes God will allow us to hurt while He shows His outrageous love to another. And it doesn't seem fair! Everything within us cries out for justice as we try to wrap our minds around the events playing out before us, and a God, who is supposed to love and care, seems unwilling to move on our behalf. He seldom answers the "whys," but He does give us His presence. If somehow we can continue to run toward Him instead of the other direction, He slowly begins to heal the hurts, and give us a greater revelation of Himself in the process!

Love today.

...as your days so shall your strength be. — Deut 33:25 NKJV

...Today, if you would hear His voice,
do not harden your hearts.... — Ps 95:78, Heb 3:7,15

LOVE IS A CHOICE

Many times in the days and years to come that commitment would be challenged. "Will you love?" And with each challenge I learned more about the amazing love and grace of God.

About a year after the hospital incident, I paced outside in front of our house. My husband had been gone for several hours, and I walked back and forth crying and praying for a long time. That first affair was over, but the same patterns were recurring. I was not in denial, as some might think, but God told me to pray and trust Him. Then I heard in my spirit, "Go to bed NOW!" I quickly obeyed, and within two to three minutes Steve pulled into the driveway.

When he walked into the house, hateful thoughts burst into my consciousness. "God, how can he do this to me?"

But once again I heard the gentle words of the Lord, "Love him."

"I can't! It's too hard! But Lord, I want to be obedient to you. You have to give me the love. I don't have it." Having learned that love is a choice — an action, much more than a warm, fuzzy feeling, I got out of bed and went into the other room to greet my husband.

Then an amazing thing happened. As I reached out my arms to embrace him, I tangibly felt as though God poured a bucket of love on top of me in a way I had never experienced. Love totally absent moments before was now overflowing. That day I discovered that love really is a Person. You can't truly love apart from Him.

But in the process of learning about God's love I also learned much about myself. On several occasions when my husband was out late I tried to imagine why.

"Maybe he was in a car accident."

Then my mind would replay the scene. An officer would come to the door with hat in hand and serious expression on his face, "Are you Mrs. Jones?"

Afraid of what he would say next, I would say, "Yes," more as a question than a reply.

"I'm sorry to inform you that your husband was in a car wreck tonight."

"Oh no! Is he okay?" I would gasp, as I grabbed the door frame for support.

Shaking his head sadly, the officer would say, "I'm sorry ma'am, he didn't make it."

The next few days would be a fog of grief as I told my children, and we would cry together. The funeral arrangements had to be made. All of our family and friends would come. One by one they would file by. It would be so, so sad. How difficult life would be alone with three children! But somehow we would survive. The resolve put strength in my backbone as I sighed deeply.

On and on the scenes would flow, but one constant would remain. A pseudo-peace would descend upon me at the thought. I would be FREE.

Then one day the Lord revealed I was actually committing murder in my heart. "Oh, God, forgive me!" I cried at the revelation. "That's awful! How could I?"

The truth is it's easy. As the Lord told Jeremiah:

The heart is hopelessly dark and deceitful, a puzzle that no one can figure out. But I, GOD, search the heart and examine the mind. I get to the heart of the human. I get to the root of things. I treat them as they really are, not as they pretend to be.
— Jeremiah 17:9,10 *The Message*

In Psalms 139:23-24, David cries out:

Search me, O God, and know my heart; Try me and know my anxious thoughts; And see if there be any hurtful way in me, And lead me in the everlasting way.

The word "hurtful" has a dual meaning.[2] It can be pain and sorrow, or an idol. When we go through trials the Lord reveals to us the thoughts and our resultant choices that continually lead us into pain and sorrow. We also begin to see the idolatrous expectations of how we think life ought to be that rule our hearts, and the things we rely on to get our needs met apart from God.

When opportunities to imagine the worst came, I learned to refocus my thoughts and choose to trust God and love instead. My future was in His hands.

PAUSE & PONDER...

1. Can you name a time when you felt others did not understand what you were experiencing?

   a. How did it make you feel?

   b. How did it affect your thoughts and actions?

2. Why do you think God consistently says to love?

3. Have you ever imagined scenarios similar to the police officer coming to the door?

4. Above we quoted David's prayer in Psalms 139:23-24, *"Search me, O God, and know my heart; Try me and know my anxious thoughts; And see if there be any hurtful way in me, And lead me in the everlasting way."*

   Again, "hurtful" means pain and sorrow or idol. Can you also ask the Lord to search your heart and reveal to you any:

   • Thoughts and choices that are leading you into ways of pain and sorrow.
   • Idolatrous expectations of how you think life ought to be.
   • Things you rely on to get your needs met apart from God.

   If He revealed anything to you, pray:

"Lord, I ask you to forgive me for the thoughts of _____
I have entertained and choices I have made to _____
that have led me in ways of pain and sorrow. I choose to bring my thoughts and choices into agreement with Your Word.

"I also ask you to forgive me for my idolatrous expectations of how I think life ought to be, particularly, the expectation that ___ _____. I choose to believe that I can expect good things from You, because You are good, even though I don't understand how You are working in my life at this present moment.

"Lord, I confess that I have relied on _____ to get some of my needs met apart from You. I'm sorry. I choose to put my hope and dependence in You.

Continue to search me and know my heart so I can walk in Your paths and receive all the goodness You have for me. My future is in Your hands."

---

[1] Not his real name. He has graciously given me permission to share our story so it can help others.
[2] *Strong's* #6090

❧ 7 ❧
Trip to the Beach

"Marilyn, would you and your family like to use our timeshare at the beach this weekend?" asked the pastor of the church where I worked.

"Oh, that sounds wonderful! I'll check and see!"

Steve was unavailable, but he encouraged me to go ahead. My friend Sherry was eager for the opportunity to get away, so we made the necessary arrangements, and arrived on a Friday night.

After we had a bite to eat and tucked our children in bed, we sat quietly reading for a period of time.

"Talk to Sherry about her relationship with Jesus." The words that began on the way to the beach continued to invade my thoughts, as I sat with Bible in hand in the stillness of the living room. "I don't know how!" I argued inwardly with the Lord, "Besides, this is supposed to be a fun time away!"

But the impressions grew stronger. Finally, I could avoid it no longer. "All right, all right, I'll do it!" I had to say something. But what?!

I knew Sherry's relationship with her husband was difficult at times. "Maybe if I somehow try to identify with her, we can approach the subject," I thought to myself. So I blurted out, "You know, Steve and I have had some difficulties in our marriage."

There I said it! That wasn't so hard!

My friend quickly responded, "Yes, I know, we've been having an affair."

My heart sank, and I was temporarily frozen. "Oh God, this can't be happening! You must have faith in me that I won't kill her!"

Now it all made sense! It had been several years since that first affair, but the day before I told my pastor I felt something was wrong, and now I knew why. Then a strange peace settled over me that could have only come from God. I was amazed at my own response to Sherry. Somehow, even in the pain, my heart was filled with compassion for this young woman who sat before me. For the next several hours we talked and made things right between the two of us.

But later when everyone else was asleep, the weight of it all settled on me like a suffocating fog. Tears poured forth unbidden from my eyes and drenched my pillow. Wrenching sobs shook me as the years of my husband's unfaithfulness, and my feelings of rejection and abandonment passed through my tormented mind. Then other scenes surfaced as though I were watching a movie screen of my life: the first grade teacher who pulled my hair, the friend who blamed me for a bike wreck I didn't cause…then darker images and wounds long buried came to the surface.

"Why, Lord? Why?!"

The sobbing continued with heaves of pain until I thought all my insides would come out. Then finally in the wee hours of the morning, feeling utterly spent, I felt the sweet presence of the Lord, as though He were wrapping His gentle arms around me, bringing comfort and peace to my troubled soul. Receiving His love as I slowly breathed in and out, I put my hand under my head and my weary body fell into a deep sleep.

"Trust in Him at all times, O people;
Pour out your heart before him…." — Psalm 62:8

Amazingly, with the dawning of a new day, Sherry, the girls, and I had a great time at the beach, but as we approached home, heaviness settled in the car. I knew I had to confront Steve. He was not surprised that the affair had been revealed. In fact, he was somewhat relieved. He promised he would get some counseling. And he did.

I did make it clear that I would not stay if it happened again. But even as the words came out of my mouth, I knew I would forgive, because long ago I determined I would be a forgiving person. It was not just about what he chose to do, but about who I wanted to be. I would forgive, but **if changes did not take place**—if there was no evidence that his repentance was sincere—**relationship could not continue**. Inwardly I cried out, "Lord, you have to protect my heart and set my boundaries!"

And He did.

STAY TENDER-HEARTED

After a painful season of processing what had occurred, things were much better for a time. The delightful, gifted man I married was back! But then as life pressures intensified as they inevitably do, Steve again distanced himself emotionally, then physically. He moved to the basement of the house and withdrew more from family life, while consistently denying involvement with other women.

"Lord, what do you want me to do?" I pleaded. Health issues that doctors attributed to stress challenged me, and the constant tension in the air was tangible.

"You don't want to hear," He said, "It's time to leave."

Maybe I didn't want to hear. After Steve's first affair ten years before, the Lord told me I could leave if I wanted, but I would be happier if I stayed. So I did. Now He was saying something different. Although it was difficult, I realized God had set my boundaries. It *was* time to go. I could never change Steve, and my own changes had never seemed enough. It was time to let God deal with us both individually. So my children and I moved out.

During that time of separation the Lord made very real to me a section of scripture in Ephesians 4:32, *"Be kind to one another, tender-hearted, forgiving each other, just as God in Christ also has forgiven you."*

I thought, "I can be kind—I'm a nice person, I can even be forgiving, I've had lots of practice." But God wanted me to be tender-hearted! That is so difficult when you've been hurt! Tender-heartedness was like the filling in a sandwich holding together two pieces of bread. I knew without it I could be kind, but still withhold my heart. I could forgive, but determine "you'll never hurt me again!"

My desperate cry was, "Lord, help me be tender-hearted!"

Several months later my husband repented to God and wanted to work on our marriage. Honestly, I didn't know if I wanted to. For the first time in many years I felt like there was life outside the pain I had lived in for so long. After a long wrestling match with the Lord, I finally chose to trust again. So we decided to go away for the weekend to try to repair our relationship. When we almost reached our destination, Steve said, "There's something I need to confess. I have been having an affair with another woman for the past two years."

After giving a few more details, he gave a sigh of relief. The truth was finally out.

But my body tensed with fierce anxiety, as I felt the crushing weight of his words, the twist of the knife in my heart. "Lord, this is too much! I can't do this any more! I'm not *that* nice! When does it end?" I screamed on the inside. But the words echoed in my heart, "Be kind… tender-hearted… forgiving…." I strained to pull myself up to ground level and respond with love, although my heart was still breaking and mind churning in a sea of doubts and fears.

The next day we went to a local church service together. Imagine my surprise when the pastor used as his sermon text, *"Be kind to one another, tender-hearted, forgiving each other, just as God in Christ also has forgiven you."*

It's amazing how relentless the Lord is when He wants to communicate a truth to us!

"Yes, Lord, I get the message!"

I tried to keep my heart tender toward God and Steve as he asked for forgiveness once more.

Forgive?! In the natural, impossible! But with God's grace, yes, I would forgive.

It would be great to say that from that point on life was wonderful, and we lived happily ever after. But not long afterward, my husband walked away from the God he thought wanted more than he could give and left me for the last time.

To the natural mind it would seem such a waste. Why continue to forgive when it's going to end anyway?

But, "in order to experience freedom we must set our own captives free."

That sounds so great, so lofty, so ideal. But it's not easy. It hurts. It's much easier to have a hard heart than a tender one. When you're hard you can't be hurt!

Or can you?

PAUSE & PONDER…

1. Knowing this story, If you were to meet Sherry or Steve for the first time, how would you react toward them inwardly? Outwardly?

2. What do you think about the statement, "It was not just about what he chose to do, but about who I wanted to be"?

3. Is there anyone you have difficulty being tender-hearted toward?

4. Ezekiel 36:26 says, *"…I will give you a new heart and put a new spirit within you; and I will remove the heart of stone from your flesh and give you a heart of flesh."* What are some characteristics of a stony heart?

   A heart of flesh?

5. Can you identify some of your fears associated with being tender hearted? Ask the Lord to help you come up with a plan of action to face these fears in a practical way.

☙ 8 ❧
A Troubling Conversation

"Lord, how many times shall I forgive my brother when he sins against me? Shall I forgive seven times?" Peter asked Jesus (Matthew 18:21).

Surely, Peter thought he was being generous. Seven times is gracious indeed! Imagine his surprise when Jesus said not seven times but seventy times seven![1]

Then Jesus told a story of a king who wanted to settle accounts with his servants, and a man who owed him ten thousand talents was brought to him. This would have been more than he could ever pay back in his lifetime. Since he was not able to pay, the master ordered that he and his wife and his children and all that he had be sold to repay the debt.

Wait a minute! That doesn't seem fair! The wife and children sold into slavery to pay back *his* debt?

Fair? No. But common practice. The widow woman with the jar of oil experienced this in Elisha's day when creditors came to take her sons into slavery to pay back the debts of her dead prophet husband (2 Kings 4:1:7). Clearly, our choices can have devastating effects on our families.

Jesus continued:

So the slave fell to the ground and prostrated himself before him, saying, 'Have patience with me and I will repay you everything.' And the lord of that slave felt compassion and released him and forgave him the debt.

But that slave went out and found one of his fellow slaves who owed him a hundred denarii[2]; and he seized him and began to choke him, saying, "Pay back what you owe." So his fellow slave fell to the ground and began to plead with him, saying, "Have patience with me and I will repay you." But he was unwilling and went and threw him in prison until he should pay back what was owed.

So when his fellow slaves saw what had happened, they were deeply grieved and came and reported to their lord all that had happened. Then summoning him, his lord said to him, "You wicked slave, I forgave you all that debt because you pleaded with me. Should you not also have had mercy on your fellow slave, in the same way that I had mercy on you?"

And his lord, moved with anger, handed him over to the torturers until he should repay all that was owed him.
My heavenly Father will also do the same to you, if each of you does not forgive his brother from your heart.

           — Matthew 18:26-35

Peter must have been shocked at the words of his master. The message was unmistakable. "If I don't forgive, I will be thrown to the tormentors!" Hard words. Crushing words. Could he receive them? *Would* he receive them?

What about Jesus? Was He thinking back to a time many centuries before?

King Zedekiah and His people made a covenant to forgive the debts of their slaves and let them go free as the law prescribed, but then changed their minds and enslaved them once again. The Lord, through the prophet Jeremiah, told them that He had made a covenant with their forefathers that every seven years they would set their servants free. But they did not obey Him. Now this generation was also breaking their covenant.

The heart of God was grieved, as it always is when He sees man's cruelty to man.

If they wanted slavery, they would experience it for themselves.

If they wanted to oppress, they would also come under the rule of the oppressor (Jeremiah 34:13-16).

God allowed the Children of Israel to come under Babylonian captivity for seventy years, even as the man in the story was turned over to the jailers to be tormented, because they refused to honor their covenant with God. Second Chronicles 36:20-21 tells us that the seventy years was one year for each Sabbath (or seventh) Year that was not honored. (See also Leviticus 26:15, 33-34.)

Seventy times seven.

Did the heart of Jesus ache? Would the people He loved ever learn the cost of unforgiveness? Did they have any idea the price He would soon pay to buy their freedom? Shortly they would all forsake Him. Would He forgive?

Yes, for this purpose He came. In fact, even now it was time to set His face toward Jerusalem. He turned and began walking.

WHAT'S IT WORTH?

Peter asked, "How many times shall I forgive?" and Jesus used an illustration about money. Actually, Jesus talked a lot about money — about profit and loss, the importance of getting a return on an investment, and to count the cost of following Him. (See Matthew 16:26; 25:14-30, Luke 14:26-33.)

"What does it profit a man if he gains the whole world and forfeits his soul" (Mark 8:36)? What does it profit if I make this guy pay and lose my own freedom?

The moments and hours of our lives are traded for purchasing power — the ability to get our needs and desires met. We earn wages, or receive a gift, inheritance, or loan. But someone will pay. For everything there is a cost.

When we bought our first house we went to the bank to request a loan. One of the first things they asked was for proof of our earning power, and a list of our assets, so they could determine our ability to pay back the debt.

But this man owed a debt he could never repay in his lifetime!

What kind of banker would ever loan him that much money? Was he foolish, or kind and generous? Your answer will help determine how easy it is for you to forgive others.

In Luke 17:1-10 we see this same question of forgiveness expressed. Jesus first told the disciples that offenses would come, and offenders deserved punishment. But then He goes on to say:

If your brother sins, rebuke him; and if he repents, forgive him. And if he sins against you seven times a day, and returns to you seven times, saying, "I repent," forgive him.

The disciples couldn't believe their ears. They cried out, "That will take more faith than we've got! *'Increase our faith!'"*

Jesus said, "*If you had faith like a mustard seed, you would say to this mulberry tree, 'Be uprooted and be planted in the sea'; and it would obey you.*"

It seems like the writer of Luke then goes on to another illustration. But I believe Jesus was continuing His thought. He tells the story of a servant who labors all day in the field. When he returns in the evening, he doesn't sit down and relax. Instead he waits on his master, and says, "*I am an unprofitable servant. I have only done what is required.*"

I think Jesus was saying, "Guys, it's not an issue of faith, you have enough faith available to you. You've not been called to a life of comfort, but to radical obedience and service to God. People may sin against you, but these are the very ones He sent me to reach! When you love them, you love the Master. When you serve them, you serve the great King. When you forgive you are not entitled to a special reward. You are only doing what I asked you to do."

Forgiveness only brings us up to zero in the account books. Forgive—you will be forgiven. People who are always concerned about keeping the ledger even, who spend their currency of time looking back at their losses, never enter a place of being profitable. Everything is about "you owe me," or "I owe you." It's a poverty mentality, a slave mindset.

Jesus has not called us to be slaves, but friends (John 15:15)! However, we do not get to enter into the full benefits of friendship as long as we are trying to keep the ledger settled in our own strength. Here is a truth we must face:

WE ALL OWE A DEBT WE CANNOT PAY

After Steve's first affair I smugly said, "I could never do anything like that!" However, a short time later, when I went to a friend for advice and he made advances toward me, I became emotionally involved. I found myself making decisions that were against everything I ever believed or conceived possible, and the inner turmoil was excruciating. I identified with Paul, *"For what I am doing, I do not understand; for I am not practicing what I would like to do, but I am doing the very thing I hate"* (Romans 7:15).

Because I had always been a good little Christian girl, it was much more difficult to forgive myself than my husband! The discovery that I too was capable of sinning in such a way was a very painful revelation!

We compare ourselves among ourselves. We say, "His sin is worse than mine. He doesn't deserve to be forgiven." Accusations fly. We judge one another. Or, we judge ourselves and try to work harder. But the truth is we can never work our way to God. We can't TRY HARDER. We will never be able to repay all the kindness the Great King has given us!

So why do we try? We just can't believe the King is that good, kind, or generous!

Jesus was softly shouting, "Don't you get it, Peter? God is good! His accounting system is much different than yours. His grace much greater! You can't repay the debt! The King never expected you to! Peter, to understand grace, you must first have a revelation of what the Father is *really* like! That's why I'm here." (See John 14:9.)

PAUSE & PONDER…

1. An offense is "something that causes displeasure, humiliation, anger, resentment, or hurt."[3]

   Do you find it more difficult to forgive offenses against you, or against those you love?

2. Has anyone ever paid a debt for you that you couldn't pay?

   What was your emotional response toward that person?

   Yourself?

   God?

3. Are there some ways you have tried to earn God's favor? If so, how?

4. Are you tired of keeping score in relationships? (I owe you…you owe me….) Ask the Lord to show you what you can do differently. Journal what you discover. (See **Journaling Tips**, in back of book, if needed.)

---

[1] Some versions say seventy-seven, but the literal Greek means seventy times seven.

[2] Probably a few days wages

[3] *Encarta Dictionary: English* (North America)

❧ 9 ❧
Who's Going to Pay?

So, if the king never expected the servant to pay back the debt, why did he come to settle the account? Because the debt still had to be paid. He was still a righteous king with holy requirements.

Through the Children of Israel God demonstrated how impossible it is to pay our own debt! God gave Moses the law so we could understand His holy requirements. There was only one problem—they couldn't keep the law, and the sacrifices for sin only postponed judgment. Yet God showed His mercy and kindness time and time again, because He was looking forward to the day when once and for all their debt would be forgiven!

When I was quite young I wanted some candy, so I walked down to Phil's Market a couple blocks away. There was only one problem. I didn't have any *real* money. Instead, I clutched in my small fist a round metal disk about the size of a nickel. I found it on the ground, and thought maybe Phil wouldn't notice that it didn't have the normal imprint on it. So, I picked out about five cents worth of penny candy (Now my age is showing, isn't it?), and took it to the counter. Hesitantly, I handed my "money" to Phil. He took a look at it, then turned to me and said very graciously, "I'm sorry, honey, this isn't money. It's a plug nickel. You can't buy anything with this."

My face got hot with shame and disappointment. "Okay, I'm sorry," I quietly said, and then turned and walked the two blocks back home.

When I arrived, my father could see there was a problem, because the shame was written on my face.

"What's wrong?" he asked.

There was no way I could tell him the whole truth, so I held out my hand with the plug nickel in it, and said with quivering lip, "I found this on the ground, and thought it was a nickel so I went to the store to buy some candy, and I couldn't." By now tears were trickling down my face. I really didn't want to lie—I knew better—but I was too ashamed to admit the truth.

Then my dad gave me a hug, took a dime from his pocket, and said, "Let's go back."

So we did, not with worthless metal, but a coin that had the imprint of the U.S. government backing up its value. The actual worth of the raw material may have been fairly comparable, but without the imprint the plug nickel was useless.

My father gave mercy to me even when I didn't deserve it. In fact, I got double what I originally wanted! That's like God's mercy found in Isaiah 61:7, "*You will receive a double measure of wealth instead of your shame. You will sing about your wealth instead of being disgraced...You will have everlasting joy.*" But I couldn't fully enjoy the blessing because I never told my dad the truth. Although he paid my candy debt, I always wondered if my father's love would have covered the cost of my dishonesty. Would he still accept me?

In retrospect, I'm sure he would have. He may have been disappointed, but he would have forgiven me.

When we are dishonest in our relationships, we are afraid people will not accept us if they know the truth about us. When we are honest and receive grace from others we learn to trust in the mercy and grace of God.

Although I learned to not tell bold-faced lies, fear of rejection kept me from being fully honest in other areas, and I carried a heavy weight of guilt and shame for many years. As a result, it was difficult for me to receive God's forgiveness. Similarly, the man in the story did not believe that the king had paid his debt; he thought it was merely postponed.

If my debt is just postponed, someday I will have to pay. Therefore, what you owe me is critical; I must collect so I can take care of my own debt. The problem is my good works and own efforts are like my plug nickel—they can never pay the debt.

CHRIST PAID THE DEBT—YOURS AND MINE.

On the cross Jesus took all the sins — past, present, and those yet to be committed — upon Himself. He went to the place of torment for us. He paid the price we could never repay! What an amazing, awesome truth! "Christ paid my debt in full."

Let the words sink in: "I don't have to pay! He's done it!"

But it doesn't stop there.

WE MUST RECEIVE GRACE AND GIVE IT.

Jesus demonstrated for us what true forgiveness does when we are fully honest with Him — **it enables us to forgive ourselves**, so we can be free of that weight of guilt and shame. But then we must also give grace to others.

Have you discovered life is not fair? We all end up with:

- UNMET NEEDS (something good should have come to us that didn't)

- UNHEALED HURTS (something bad shouldn't have happened to us but did)

- UNRESOLVED ISSUES (our inability to process those needs and hurts in a positive manner).[1]

Do you want fair? The law is fair. If you take my eye, I take your eye, if you take my tooth, I take your tooth (Exodus 21:23,24; Matthew 5:38,39). If you're unfaithful to me, you die (See Leviticus 20:10). Sounds fair to me!

But are you sure you want to live by the law?

Jesus said that if you even look on someone with lust in your heart, you are guilty of adultery (Matthew 5:27-28), or if you hate someone you're equal to a murderer (Matthew 5:20-24, 1 John 3:15).

James 2:10 says further, *"For whoever keeps the whole law and yet stumbles in one point, he has become guilty of all."*

"Are you saying if I entertain bad thoughts I'm just as bad as the guy on death row?"

I didn't say it, God did. It's quite a dilemma, isn't it?! But there's hope!

We can choose if we are going to live by the law or by grace. Under the law, we all deserve to die. But Christ fulfilled the just requirements of the law so we could live in the kingdom where grace is in place. Here, if you take my eye, I don't take your eye. I give you GRACE. If you take my tooth, I don't get even. I give you GRACE.

Satan can't understand grace, and he can't touch me here. So what does he do? He tries to get me to step back under the law when someone offends or hurts me.

It's easy to talk about grace in lofty, noble terms, when it's my little sins. But when you hurt me, those lofty thoughts fly right out the window!

I want grace for me, but JUSTICE for YOU!

Revelation 12:10 says that Satan is always bringing accusations against people, *"…the accuser of our brethren has been thrown down, he who accuses them before our God day and night."* God will not hear accusations unless they are established by two or three witnesses.[2] We either agree with Satan's testimony by clinging to our demands for justice, or we agree with the testimony of Jesus. He made sufficient payment for our sins and the sins of those who hurt us.

Also, if we refuse to forgive, we come under a curse, because we can't keep the law that we demand of others. *"Cursed is everyone who does not abide by **all things** written in the book of the law, to perform them."* (Galatians 3:10, emphasis mine; see also Deuteronomy 27:26.)

Since we have stepped back under the law, now Satan, the one with whom we've come into agreement against someone else, has a right to bring accusation against us! *"…In the way you judge, you will be judged…"* (Matthew 7:2; Luke 6:37).

Deuteronomy 28 talks about some of the effects of living under a curse. They can be summarized as follows:

- Humiliation
- Barrenness
- Unfruitfulness

- Mental and physical sickness
- Family breakdown
- Poverty
- Defeat
- Oppression
- Failure
- God's disfavor.[3]

Some of the symptoms may be:

- Physical—such as headaches, digestive disorders, back pain, arthritis, or cancer[4]
- Emotional—which may manifest as anger, fear, jealousy, disdain, mental torment, or depression
- Relational—which causes separation from family members or avoidance of certain people
- Spiritual—which results in separation from God, lack of desire to spend time with Him, feelings of condemnation, and inability to receive love
- Addictions—our attempt to escape the pain of any of these curses.

Like sin—judgments, bitterness, and unforgiveness will take you further than you want to go, cost you more than you want to pay, and keep you longer than you want to stay.

PAUSE & PONDER...

1. Read these verses and then answer the following questions:

    Mark 11:25-26 *"Whenever you stand praying, forgive, if you have anything against anyone, so that your Father who is in heaven will also forgive you your transgressions. But if you do not forgive, neither will your Father who is in heaven forgive your transgressions."*

    Matthew 5:23-24 *"...if you are presenting your offering at the altar, and there remember that your brother has something against you, leave your offering there before the altar and go; first be reconciled to your brother, and then come and present your offering."*

    a. Is forgiveness only applied to people who repent?

    b. Why is it important to pursue reconciliation with someone who has a problem with you?

2. Are there any symptoms listed above you may be currently experiencing.

3. Are there any areas where you do not feel fully forgiven by God? If so, write down those areas on a piece of paper and present them to the Lord in prayer.

4. Do you have friends with whom you can be truly honest, who love and accept you, and help you receive God's acceptance and forgiveness?

---

[1] Liberty Savard, *Breaking the Power* (Bridge Logos Publishers, 1997, 2000)

[2] Deuteronomy 17:6; Matthew 18:16; 2 Corinthians 13:1; 1 Timothy 5:19; Hebrews 10:28

[3] Derek Prince, *Blessing or Curse: You Can Choose* (Chosen Books, 1990), 43

[4] These physical ailments may have other causes as well, but bitterness has been medically linked to them.

The Acorn

You can't see it, the little acorn in my pocket.
I feel the smooth nut and textured cap,
As my fingers gently caress it.
At times during the day, I never know when,
I feel a little prick from the point on the end.
So, I bring it out and before my eyes
The cap comes off, branches grow,
And leaves spread far and wide —
This grand yet bitter tree defies the axe of man!
"I can't hold it! There's too much pain!"
I cry on the one hand.
But on the other, I'm filled with a strange sort of glee
As Anger and Hurt, my secret friends,
Come out to play with me.
On the stage we've created high in the limbs
Over and over we re-enact
The same familiar scenes.
Then I fold in the branches when I tire of them,
Put the cap on the acorn,
And stuff it in my pocket again.
But when I do, bitter roots grow deep.
They spring up here and spring up there,
Entwining friends and family.
But my eyes are blinded, I refuse to see.
After all, it's just a little acorn.
What harm can it be?

— Marilyn Hume

～ 10 ～
You Owe Me!

Let's just suppose one day I see Sam who hurt me in some way. I grab him by the shirt collar and get my face within inches of his, and begin to speak with intensity.

"You did not meet my expectations!"

"I thought I was marrying a prince and ended up with warts on my lips."

Or, if I was a guy, and this was Samantha, it could be, "I thought I was marrying Cinderella and ended up with the wicked stepmother!"

Or, "You stole from me..."

"You took a job I was supposed to have."

"You ruined my ministry!"

"You promised to pay me back!"

Or, maybe the voice isn't raised. Maybe there's just a great sense of pain and disappointment, "You weren't the child I thought I would have."

"You took my self-respect."

"You stole my innocence."

"You promised to love me."

"You didn't meet my needs."

"You should have kept me safe!"

"You should have known what was going on."

"You hurt me."

"I was only a kid."

The anger rises again, "You owe me!"

Then I throw him into a cage—the prison of my judgments—and lock the door. There's only one problem: this cage is attached to me, clutched firmly in my grasp, so wherever I go, he goes.

But he's such a good slave! At a moment's notice, in my mind he can quickly replay the evil deed again and again.

I want to step into grace, but my judgmental attitudes keep pulling me down. If I continue to judge, two things will happen:

1) I will be judged.

Sometimes when people judge us, we don't have to look too far back in our history to discover that we have recently judged someone else! I hate it when that happens!

God will not violate His own laws. We will reap what we sow. If we judge we will be judged. God created seeds to have within them the power of multiplication. If I sow one little seed of judgment, I don't get just one seed in return, but the potential of hundreds of seeds! God's laws can either work for us or against us! We get to choose!

If I refuse to forgive, not only will I be judged, also:

2) I will be tormented.

Anger, bitterness, physical ailments, feelings of unworthiness, and so on, are all tormentors that affect not only us, but those around us.

WHAT'S WRONG WITH THIS CAR?

Not long ago I went outside my office to start my car. I turned the key and heard a groaning sound. I suspected my battery was in the throes of death, although there had been no previous indication. Sure enough, when a friend connected jumper cables to it, the car immediately started. I stopped on the way home to have the battery replaced. But the next day my speedometer quit working, so I went back to the shop. They checked and said there was no correlation. The day after that my "service engine soon" light came on.

There had been a series of odd things happen to the car recently. About nine months earlier my power steering cable broke. I got it repaired, and then the cruise control stopped working. No big deal, I could live with that. Shortly thereafter I tried to shift the car into gear and nothing happened. At the recommendation of a mechanic who thought it was the ignition release switch, I stuck a round corndog stick into a thing-a-ma-jig hole by the gear shift. It worked, although it looked strange! Other than these minor inconveniences, the car ran beautifully.

But with these recent failures I felt insecure about the reliability of my vehicle. It was time for another visit to a repair shop. All systems were saying, "Do something!" But I didn't know what!

The mechanic's findings surprised me. The issues were all related. My old battery had leaked acid on a cable… drip…drip…drip… until it ate through a wire, and then started corroding the computer board on my car.

Bitterness is like that! If unattended it will spill over and slowly eat through the control wires of our life, causing damage to ourselves, and possibly others. Hebrews 12:15 gives us some life-giving advice, _"See to it that no one comes short of the grace of God; that no root of bitterness springing up causes trouble, and by it many be defiled."_

For some time medical doctors have recognized the profound affect that anger, bitterness, and other negative emotions have on our bodies, confirming the Word of God spoken thousands of years ago.

DOWN-PAYMENT ON A HEALING

The man was obviously crippled from the rheumatoid arthritis that had taken its toll in his body. He responded at a training seminar several years ago when the leader asked for those who needed prayer to come forward.

The group I was in had him sit down in a chair prayed for a few moments. We were amazed to see the immediate effects of God's work in his body. As we continued to pray for more healing, the Lord gently whispered in my spirit, "Ask him about his relationship with his father." Brave person that I am, I just stood there praying silently. After all, I was the only woman in this group of several men praying with him.

"Maybe one of them will say something," I thought to myself.

But the words came stronger, "Ask him about his relationship with his father."

I glanced up and caught the eyes of a man standing next to me. The look on his face was unmistakable. "You have something, say it!"

So I did. "How was your relationship with your father?"

"He's dead."

"That's okay. What was your relationship like?"

"Well, I guess it wasn't good. I was the black sheep in the family."

Then I spoke as I felt the Lord instructed, "God has given you a down-payment on your healing today. Now He wants you to go back home and work through forgiveness of your father and yourself, so He can complete in you what He has begun."[1]

The man agreed to do so, and with grateful heart, he walked away a little straighter, hope rekindled in the King who is very, very good.

Nearly every week I pray with people who are experiencing torment in their bodies or relationships with God and others because they are dragging around these cages of bitter judgments. For some, if you open the cage you find not just one person, but another, and another, and another—a seeming inexhaustible supply of people who have hurt them through the years! What a heavy, unbearable burden!

SO, WHO IS PAYING FOR THESE CLUTCHED FISTS?

Here is Sam, in this prison that I drag along behind me. I may even say the words, "I forgive you," but I just can't let go. I can keep him back here out of sight, and function quite well for a period of time. Then, if for some reason I happen to turn around and see him, immediately my stomach churns, and thoughts of anger and revenge well up. Or again I feel the deep hurt and want to cry or run. Maybe I bury it deep within once more.

Either way, I refuse to allow God to heal. Why? Because I don't really trust God to bring justice, and I want my offender to pay! He hurt me!

But there is another price to be paid. Because I am clutching so tightly to my right to get even, this prison of my judgments, the hurt that refuses to heal, my hands are full. I can't receive everything that God desires to give me.

TIME OUT

Before we go any further, let's take a look at the "Sams" in your life. As we mentioned earlier, we all end up with unmet needs (something good should have to come to you that didn't), unhealed hurts (something bad shouldn't have happened to you but did), and unresolved issues (you are unable to process those needs and hurts in a positive manner).

Are there people who you feel owe you something in any of these areas? These may be people who invoke thoughts of bitterness, revenge, anger, avoidance, hurt, disappointment, etc. They may not be people who hurt you or someone you love, but those who did nothing to prevent it. Ask the Holy Spirit to bring them to mind.

The person you may have the most difficulty forgiving is yourself. Are there things you have done, mistakes you have made, or unattained perfection that keep you from accepting God's grace?

What about God? Have you taken offense toward Him? Have you become more focused on what He hasn't done for you than what He has?

Can you identify what you feel is owed to you? What do you feel you lost? The debt could be loss of relationships with friends or family, self-esteem, respect or recognition by others, emotional happiness, job benefits, finances, physical abilities or mobility, dreams, direction, trust in God, etc. Whether the losses are real or perceived is not important.

Take some time to grieve these losses. It may take longer than this session, but there are some things you can do to help the process.

In John 14:16, Jesus says, _"...I will pray the Father, and He shall give you another Comforter, that He may abide with you for ever_ (KJV)." The very presence of God is with us through this Comforter, the Holy Spirit. Now, talk to God about the losses, and who you feel caused them, just like you would talk to a friend. Tell Him how you feel. Pour out the hurt and pain. Release the anger. For some, this will be easy. For others, it will be very difficult because you're used to stuffing that anger. When you feel like there is no more to express, allow the Father to comfort you through the power of the Holy Spirit. It may help to imagine yourself climbing up into His lap and allowing Him to hold you. Experience it. Receive His peace. There's more to be done, but He is with you in this stage of the process. Then give Him thanks. There's some good news ahead!

...Weeping may last for the night,
But a shout of joy comes in the morning. —Psalm 30:5

PAUSE & PONDER...

1. If you have not already done so, identify the "Sams" in your life. Ask the Holy Spirit to bring them to mind. (See subtitle "Time Out.") Remember to include yourself or God.

2. Identify the debts you feel they owe. What do you feel you lost?

   - Relationships with friends or family
   - Self-esteem
   - Esteem or recognition by others
   - Emotional happiness
   - Job benefits
   - Finances
   - Physical abilities or mobility
   - Dreams
   - Direction
   - Trust in God
   - Other

3. Take some time to grieve these losses as stated in this chapter:

- Tell the Father how you feel
- Pour out your hurt and pain
- Release the anger, "Lord, I am angry that…"
- Allow the Father to comfort you through the power of the Holy Spirit
- Receive His peace
- Give Him thanks.

---

[1] Our purpose is never to accuse people that it is their fault they do not get healed. However, as stated in a Chapter 9 footnote, there is much medical evidence that negative emotions do have damaging effects on our bodies. Also, we know from scripture that sin and unforgiveness will hinder our prayers. In this particular case the Lord gave me a word of knowledge about the man's relationship with his father. A word of knowledge, as mentioned in 1 Corinthians 12:8, is supernatural revelation by the Holy Spirit of circumstances, problems, solutions, etc, that come through impressions, visions, or dreams. There are many examples of words of knowledge given to men in the Bible, such as Genesis 6:13; 2 Kings 8:11-12; Acts 8:17-23; 9:1-21; 10:1-48; 11:28; and 21:10-15, to name a few.

It is very important that any time we pray for people we make them feel more loved and cared for by God, rather than accusing them of sin, bitterness, lack of faith, etc. If God does reveal something through a word of knowledge, it is much more effective to ask questions, such as, "I know God loves you so much and wants to answer your prayers. Are you aware of anything that may hinder your prayers, such as unconfessed sin, or someone you may need to forgive?" This gives people the opportunity to search their own hearts without feeling attacked. If they can't think of anything, we graciously pray for their healing and revelation of more of God's love and kindness. When people feel secure in God's love and ours, it is easier to deal with these difficult issues. Romans 2:4 says it is the kindness of God that leads us to repentance.

～ 11 ～
So, How Good is He?

It's time to take a deep breath. We've been digging deep. Before we can fully release our tightly clutched fists, we want to know something:

- How trustworthy is God?
- Why did He allow all these bad things to happen?
- Yes, I've heard that we live in a fallen world, and bad things happen to good people, but why me?
- What did I do to deserve this?
- If He won't answer these questions, how can I trust Him?
- How good is this King?

We've all heard election campaign promises that sound so good when spoken, but are seldom realized. Now in fairness to politicians, they don't have control over everything. Most are sincere when the promises are made, but honestly, they don't have all the power to carry them out.

Is God just a pump-you-up politician, or is He really as good as He says He is?

Moses asked if He could see God's glory, and the Lord said, *"I Myself will make all My goodness pass before you…"* (Exodus 33:19). His goodness! This is the essence of who God is—the glory of His nature and personhood. He is GOOD!

Let's pause for a few moments and take a look at some of the things He has promised He will do for you. Many of these promises were made specifically to the Children of Israel, but the principles remain the same for us, since in Jesus Christ, we also are heirs to all the promises made to Abraham concerning his offspring (Galatians 3:29).

♦ My child, **I promise to restore you to health and heal all the wounds that life has inflicted upon you.** You will no longer fear, but enjoy abundant peace and security. It's time for payback. Those years of loss you have experienced, I will restore. I will refresh you and satisfy your desires with good things, and cause you to soar on wings as a young eagle, far above all the things that have tethered you to the earth in the past. All I ask is that you come to Me, weary and burdened child, and I will give you rest. (See Jeremiah 30:17; 33: 6; Joel 2:25; Psalm 103:5; Jeremiah 31:25; Matthew 11:28.)

♦ My child, **I promise to cleanse you from all the things that have separated you from Me.** I will forgive your sins, and wipe the record books clean. I will replace your stony, wounded heart with a new one that has single purpose, focused on Me and My awesome plans for you.

I will place My very own Spirit within you that will help you follow My decrees and inspire you to have awe and reverence of Me. My pledge to you is that I will never stop doing good to you or your children after you. All you have to do is yield to My Spirit at work within you. I will do the rest. I will form you into the person you have always wanted to be.

Do you have any idea how much joy I receive from doing good things for you? I have an inheritance prepared for you, and My entire heart and soul are fully committed to help you receive it. It's not something you can buy or earn, but simply receive as a much loved child of the King. In fact, I personally have qualified you to receive it. Let me share My joy with you. (See Jeremiah 33:8; Ezekiel 36:25-27; Jeremiah 32:39-41; Colossians 1:12; John 16:24.)

♦ **I promise to contend with those who contend with you, and I will save your children,** both physical and spiritual. You have no need to fear, for I will be with you. I will bring your children back from the north, south, east, and west. I personally will contend with those who try to hold them in captivity. I will pour My Spirit upon your precious children and bless all your descendants. The more you trust in My goodness and love, the more secure they will be. (See Isaiah 49:25; 43:5-6; 44:3.)

♦ My child, **I promise to strengthen you when you are weak and help you in times of difficulty.** There is no need to fear or look anxiously about you. I will always be with you. My righteous right hand will uphold you when you think you are going to fall. Be assured, even to your old age and gray hairs I will sustain you. I will carry you when you can't walk on your own, and rescue you when there is no one else to help.

I will satisfy you with long life, preserve you, and show you the full extent of My salvation, which includes deliverance, victory, prosperity, health, and welfare.[1] My benefit plan is unrivaled! You will live in a peaceful habitation, a secure dwelling, an undisturbed resting place. As a citizen of My kingdom, You don't have to worry about what you will eat, or what you will wear. As you seek Me and obey My voice I will provide all you need. (See Isaiah 32:18; Matthew 6:25-33.)

♦ My child, **I promise to watch over you for your good, and will bring you back to the land of your inheritance.** I will build you up and not tear you down. I will plant you and not uproot you. I will give you a heart to know Me. You will be My child, and I will be your God, for you will return to Me with all your heart. I am confidently assured of this, because you will see Me for who I truly am. In the time of My favor (and that time is NOW!) I will answer you when you call. I will preserve and keep you, because I have chosen you to be My promise to the people, a visible symbol of hope, that I will restore their inheritance to them as well. (See Jeremiah 24:6-7; Isaiah 49:8.)

♦ **I also promise that when you call I will show you things that you never dreamt possible.** When you can't see a path, and don't know which way to go, I will guide you. As a shepherd looks after his scattered flock when he is with them, so will I look after you. I will turn the darkness into light before you, because I AM the Light of the

World. I will go before you and make all the rough places smooth, because I AM the Way. When you have difficulty knowing truth from error, come to Me because I AM Truth. I am your very reason for existence, because I AM Life itself, and the access point for all that the Father desperately longs to give you. (See Jeremiah 33:3; Ezekiel 34:12; Isaiah 42:16; John 8:12; John 14:6; Exodus 3:13-14.)

♦ My child, **I will turn your mourning into gladness, and give you comfort and joy instead of sorrow.** Once again women will dance and be glad. Joy will flow like wine upon the young and old men as well. I will satisfy you with abundance. You will be amazed at My goodness! You will find your joy in me, as together we ride on the heights of the earth and feast on the awesome inheritance I have prepared for you. (See Jeremiah 31:13-14; Isaiah 58:14.)

I WILL do all these things and much more if you choose to trust me.

These are not the words of a politician. They are but a few of the promises the King of Kings, and Lord of Lords has made to you as a citizen of His kingdom. He's the Creator of the universe, who causes the sun to shine by day and the moon by night, who sets the stars in their course, and the rhythmic tides of the sea.

> *The Rock! His work is perfect, For all His ways are just; A God of faithfulness and without injustice, righteous and upright is he.*
> —Deuteronomy 32:4

> *God is not a man, that He should lie, nor a son of man, that He should change His mind. Does He speak and then not act? Does He promise and not fulfill?* —Numbers 23:19 NIV

The question is not whether His words are true, but whether you will believe Him. Do you feel the things you have lost outweigh what God wants to restore? Do you need to have all your questions answered before you will trust Him? Or, will you choose to trust His character, and believe He will make sense of all the "non-sense" in

His time and way? Do you want to continue looking back on what has happened in the past, or look forward to the wonderful future God has for you?

Isaiah 55 tells us that God's ways and thoughts are higher than ours and His word will come to pass. Then He promises:

> *...you shall go out with joy, and be led out with peace; the mountains and the hills shall break forth into singing before you, and all the trees of the field shall clap their hands. Instead of the thorn shall come up the cypress tree, and instead of the brier shall come up the myrtle tree; and it shall be to the LORD for a name, for an everlasting sign that shall not be cut off.*
> —Isaiah 55:12-13 NKJV

You may have received thorns and briers in the past, but they are short-lived. Their season comes to an end. The cypress and the myrtle are evergreens that last through many generations. Trust God's ways, believe His words, let Him change your expectations, and see all of creation respond before you to bring God's promises to pass!

PAUSE & PONDER...

1. Take another look at the promises God has made above. See which one jumps out to you. Then spend a little time journaling. Ask the Lord, "What does this mean for me?"

2. Think about the question, "Do I feel the things I have lost outweigh what God wants to restore?" Then on a piece of paper make two columns. On the left side list the three greatest things you feel you have lost. Ask the Lord what He wants to restore in this area. Write what you hear in the right-hand column.

3. Ask the Lord to reveal to you any lies you may believe about His ability to bring restoration, and any fears that support these lies. Then ask Him to reveal to you the truth.

4. Make a decision, "Will I believe the lie or the truth? Will I choose to trust God?

---

[1] *Strong's #3444*

The Dance

When I was a little girl I loved to play dress-up.
My favorite outfit was a full skirt
that would spread all the way out
when I would turn in a circle.
I would twirl and twirl around with skirt billowing
until I would become quite dizzy
(which usually didn't take very long).
I always felt so pretty and special and carefree as I danced about.

Somehow on the journey to adulthood
it is easy to lose that childlike inner delight.
Outward circumstances soon dictate
whether or not we have reason to dance,
and we look to other people instead of God
for fulfillment and happiness.

For some time I felt like a girl leaning against the wall,
waiting for someone — anyone — to ask her to dance.

You can sense with me the anticipation and excitement
as she sees someone — anyone — coming close,
ready to speak…
Only to experience the disappointment
in the pit of her stomach as he moves on.
Before long she stops anticipating,
hoping, living…it is safer that way…
And the wall she is leaning against
now becomes a part of her flesh —
a cold, icy structure of fears,
broken dreams and unfulfilled promises.

"But I will court her again, and bring her into the wilderness,
and speak to her tenderly there.
There I will give back her vineyards to her,
And transform her Valley of Troubles into a Door of Hope,
She will respond to Me there,
Singing with joy as in days long ago in her youth."
—Hosea 2:14,15 TLB

Do you see Him?!

The Prince of Peace has invited me to dance!
But to do that I must let go of the wall
that has become a part of me.
I must challenge my fears,
Dare to dream again,
And realize the promises He has given me
are still alive.
I must step out and risk once more.

"Forget the former things,
do not dwell on the past
See, I am doing a new thing…" —Isaiah 43:18

"But I don't know the steps."
"I WILL TEACH YOU," He says.
"But I don't have a thing to wear."
(Girls *always* have to say that!)
"COME…I LOVE YOU JUST THE WAY YOU ARE."
"What if I make a fool of myself?"
"WHAT IF YOU DO?"
"Shouldn't we be going this way?"
"NO, I WILL LEAD YOU."
"Can we dance faster?"
He smiles, "LEAVE THE TIMING TO ME."

And as He leads, I look into His face
and am filled with awe and wonder,
and a spirit of worship...

It has been said that worship is like
reaching up and touching the face of God...

Oh God, I want to reach up and touch Your eyes,
for I know they will be full of love and compassion.
I want to touch Your mouth,
for the corners will be turned up gently in a smile,
I want to place my fingers upon Your forehead...
There will be no deep furrows of disapproval,
but little laugh wrinkles around Your eyes.
I want to reach up and feel Your ears,
that are always open to hear me when I cry,
And I want to feel the gentle breeze of Your breath
upon my hand
as You fill me afresh with Your Spirit and life.

Oh God, I want to worship You...
Emmanuel...
God with Us...
The Everlasting Father
The Prince of Peace...

You're calling us to look into Your face and dance with You.
To celebrate life...
to let go of our fears...
and with joy and abandonment risk again...

Soon others will want to join in the dance...
and together with childlike delight
we'll twirl 'round and 'round and 'round...

— Marilyn Hume
© 1993

❧ 12 ❧
Will I Give Grace?

I want to trust the Lord. I want to believe His promises, but my belief system is definitely put to the test as I stand before the one who has offended me. Is God really good? Will He keep His promises, or do I get even with my offender? Do I make him pay?

Here I am, facing Sam, the person in the prison of my bitter judgment.

What if…?

What if I were to choose grace for me AND grace for you?

What did Jesus say? "Prison…torment… My heavenly Father will also do the same to you, if each of you does not forgive his brother from your heart."

Forgive from my heart…how do I do that?

The heart has long been described as our MIND, EMOTION, and WILL. The WILL of a believer is the gate through which we choose to follow either our flesh or our spirit.

Oswald Chambers said:

> "Your will agrees with God, but in your flesh there is a nature that renders you powerless to do what you know you ought to do…What causes you to say 'I will not obey' is something less deep and penetrating than your will. It is perversity or stubbornness, and they are never in agreement with God. The most profound thing in a person is his will, not sin…In someone who has been born again, the source of the will is Almighty God. '…For it is God who works in you both to will and to do for His good pleasure'… God not only expects me to do His will, but He is in me to do it."[1]

93

The WILL involves a legal transaction, a choice. WILL I choose to forgive you, not based on my emotions, which presently may be bouncing around like a tennis ball?

What if I give you grace? What if I allow God to be your judge, not me? What if I let you out of jail? What if I open the door and let you walk free?

What if....?

AMY

Amy, with a look of shock and repulsion on her face, slid on the floor away from me and cowered against the wall. I had just said to her, "Amy, at some point you're going to have to forgive your stepfather."

"No one has ever told me that before! They've all told me he should never be forgiven!"

She was right. In man's eyes he should never be forgiven. He along with a friend had repeatedly molested her as a child. Her mother was no help either. She had abused her too! They lived in a respectable neighborhood, but no one knew what was going on behind closed doors, until one day Amy could take it no longer, and ran through a plate glass window.

Her stepfather was put in jail for a few years and she was bounced from one foster home to another until she was placed in the home of a Christian leader who also molested her. What her stepfather had done was now a well-known fact, but the truth about the Christian leader had been carefully hidden, until now as her life was quickly unraveling...

I've met with that look of shock and repulsion many times as I've talked with people about forgiveness. Forgive the unforgivable? It seems unfair, not right...impossible!

But let's continue...

WHAT IF I LET YOU GO FREE?

I am not saying that what you did is okay. But I give up my right to get even with you.

I let it go.

I forgive you.

I will not allow my judgments of you to steal my peace and joy. I will put my faith and trust in the justice, mercy and goodness of God.

You may still have to deal with consequences of your actions, but God gets to choose those consequences, not me. Physical separation may be necessary. The court system may be involved, depending upon the offense, particularly if my safety or the safety of children or others is in question.

I may still have to confront the issue. Matthew 18:15-17 gives clear guidelines about this:

> *If your brother sins, go and show him his fault in private; if he listens to you, you have won your brother. "But if he does not listen to you, take one or two more with you, so that BY THE MOUTH OF TWO OR THREE WITNESSES EVERY FACT MAY BE CONFIRMED. "If he refuses to listen to them, tell it to the church; and if he refuses to listen even to the church, let him be to you as a Gentile and a tax collector.*

God is definitely not soft on sin!

If you choose not to repent, reconciliation will not be possible now, and I may have to set firm boundaries because of your unrepentant attitude.

But will I forgive? Will I release you from my judgments? Will I allow God to be your judge, not me?

"This is *so* hard, the pain so deep!" I think to myself as you stand before me.

"What's that I see? Whose voice do I hear?"

I hear the voice of Jesus crying before an unrepentant cursing and mocking crowd, "Father, forgive them for they don't know what they do!"

But my mind wants to argue, "Yes, but, He was the Son of God! He can't expect me to forgive like that!"

Then I see Stephen on his knees outside the city as stones are hurled upon him by another unrepentant crowd. I hear a loud echo, "Lord, do not hold this sin against THEM!²"

The same Holy Spirit that was in Jesus and Stephen is now available to me. Through His power I can open the prison door.

The question is what will I choose? Will I forgive?

"Father, I…"

PAUSE & PONDER…

1. Let's take another look at the basic forgiveness principles we've covered so far. If I choose to forgive:

I will **RECALL:**
- What forgiveness is and what it isn't
  - o It is not saying that what you did is okay.
  - o It is not removing consequences of your actions, but God gets to choose those consequences not me.
  - o It is not trust. Trust has to be earned in process.
  - o It is not reconciliation. That is only possible through repentance and restoration of relationship.
  - o It is caring for you enough to confront your actions if needed.
  - o It is caring for myself enough to set up appropriate boundaries if you are unwilling to change.
- What I am forgiving specifically.
- What I have lost.

I will **REPENT:**
- For my lack of faith and trust in the justice, mercy, and goodness of God.
- For allowing my judgments of you to steal my peace and joy.
- For holding bitterness against you.

I will **RELEASE**:

- My grief, anger, and hurt over what I have lost.
- My judgments of you and allow God to be your judge.

Which of these principles is the greatest challenge to you? Why?

2. Look at the list of those people who you feel owe you something. Let's take them one by one. If you're ready to forgive, pray a prayer something like this:

    "Father, I thank you for being a just and fair God, and righteous in all you do. Today I choose to forgive _____ (insert name) for _____ (list offenses specifically). I release (him/her) from my judgment, and place (him/her) in Your hands. I also ask You to forgive _____ (insert same person's name), and cleanse (him/her) from (his/her) sin. Forgive me too for holding onto any anger or bitterness toward this person. I give You all the pain and hurt that I've suffered, and believe that You will bring healing to me. Thank You, Lord, for Your grace and mercy.

3. *Sit quietly and ask the Lord what He would like to give you in exchange for your bitterness, anger and pain. It may come as a word, a picture, or feeling. Receive it.*

    Then allow the Lord to embrace you with His love.

4. Now that you have chosen forgiveness, who will hold you accountable for living it out and not slipping back into bitterness?

---

[1] June 6, ***My Utmost for His Highest: An Updated Edition in Today's Language,*** by Oswald Chambers, edited by James Reimann, (Discovery House Publishers, 1992), Emphasis mine.
[2] Acts 7:60

❧ 13 ❧
ᵀ𝒽𝑒 𝒮𝑎𝒷𝒷𝑎𝓉𝒽 𝒴𝑒𝑎𝓇

You may say to yourself, "If I have forgiven I would like to think it is finished. But is it? My mind has grasped some of the validity of forgiveness. I have engaged my will and chosen to forgive, but what about my emotions? His face is still before me.

How do I walk into the same room as this person and not let him affect me? How do I keep the old feelings of hurt, anger, fear, or resentment from resurfacing?"

Before we answer that, I want to lay more ground work. This will take a few chapters, but hang with me; I believe it will be worth it!

I'm of the firm conviction that everything Jesus said and did was a fulfillment of an Old Testament principle. When He walked with the two men on the road to Emmaus after the resurrection, and later met with the disciples, He opened up the photo album of the Old Testament and showed them pictures of Himself throughout the writings of Moses, Psalms and the prophets. *Then He opened their minds to understand the Scriptures*" (Luke 24:27,44,45). The scriptures that the disciples used were the Old Testament books.

With that in mind, let's review some of what we have learned. In the seventh or Sabbath Year, servants were to be released. How did a person become a servant?

He or a family member may have sold him during times of poverty. A creditor may have taken him as a slave to repay debts. He may have been sold to make restitution for something stolen, lost or broken if he had no money to repay.

It is important to understand why we are just talking about forgiving people who may owe debts, rather than what we would term the greater sins like rape, adultery, or murder. These were normally punishable by death.

Remember, we've established that Jesus equated hatred with murder, and lust with adultery, and if we've broken one of the laws, we're guilty of breaking them all. So we all deserve death! It's not a value statement—sin is sin. It's an issue of the heart! Sin makes us all its servants. We are all in bondage, and need to be set free.

We said Jesus came to set free those who were bound. We talked about how the Children of Israel went into captivity because they refused to release their servants. That gives some context for what I am going to say next.

Deuteronomy says that when a servant was released, he was not to be sent away empty handed:

> *You shall furnish him liberally from your **flock** and from your **threshing floor** and from your **wine vat**; you shall give to him as the LORD your God has blessed you.*
> —Deuteronomy 15:14

Why these three things?

First of all, simple kindness. The servant had little of his own, he had served another. Now he needed a fresh start, and provision to go his way to establish himself free from bondage.

But there was another reason.

These three things enabled the servant to come before the Lord to have his sins forgiven and enter into covenant relationship with God. Three times a year every male, on behalf of his family, was to present himself before the Lord at the:

- Feast of Unleavened Bread, which included Passover (Pesach)
- Feast of Weeks, which included Pentecost (Shavuot)
- Feast of Tabernacles at the end of the season when the harvest was gathered (Succot)

He was not to come empty-handed, but bring from the increase of his flocks and herds, his grain, and vineyards the things needed for his sacrifices and gifts to God. (See Exodus 23:17, 29:38-46, 34:24; Numbers 1:14, 28:1-31; Deuteronomy 16:16.)

These were used as provision for the Levites, as sacrifices of the particular feast, and for the daily sacrifices.

Twice a day, year in and year out, the priests were to offer two lambs (from the **flock**) as burnt offerings, one in the morning and the other in the evening. With each lamb they were instructed to offer fine flour (from the **threshing floor**) mixed with oil as a grain offering, and wine (from the **wine vat**) as a drink offering.

These offerings were made at the entrance to the Tent of Meeting for the sins of the people. The Lord promised that as the priests did this:

... I will meet with you, to speak to you there. I will meet there with the sons of Israel, and it shall be consecrated by My glory... I will dwell among the sons of Israel and will be their God. They shall know that I am the LORD their God who brought them out of the land of Egypt, that I might dwell among them...
— Exodus 29:42-46

Let's look at the sequence in these scriptures. When the priests offered the sacrifices:

- They personally would have interactive relationship and intimacy with God
- The Lord would extend relationship to those the priest represented
- God's presence, holiness and glory would be established in that place, and
- The people would have a tangible knowledge and awareness of His presence, supernatural power, and lordship among them.

Can you see the Father's desire to not only meet and talk with, but also dwell among the people He created? Every morning, every evening, this was the passion of His heart.

"Draw near to me, because I am desperate to draw near to you! I want to reveal Myself to you!" (See James 4:8; Psalm 73:28.)

As the sweet aroma of the sacrifices went before the Lord, He looked forward to a day when once and for all His Son Jesus would be the sacrificial lamb who would take away the sins of the world so full relationship with mankind could be restored.

When we forgive, we step into two roles:

1. The **master** who releases his servant, and provides him with what he needs to come before God, and

2. The **priest** who goes before God on his behalf.

The role of the master is the legal transaction of forgiving the debt. When we step into the role of priest God begins to deal further with our mind and emotions.

PAUSE & PONDER…

1. The master was instructed to give to the servant *"as the LORD your God has blessed you."* We've talked about all you've lost. Ask the Lord to reveal the ways He has blessed you. Write them down.

2. Thank Him for His blessings. Graham Cooke says, "Give thanks until you become thanks." Repeat the things you're thankful for until your emotions catch up with your words, and you actually feel thankful.

3. Imagine what it would have been like to have the presence of the Lord manifested among the people. Ask the Lord to give you further revelation on this.

ℳ Kingdom of Priests

God's original intent was for the children of Israel to be a kingdom of priests who would bring blessing to all nations of the earth. Peter echoes that intent when he says that we have now become a royal priesthood. (See Genesis 22:18, Exodus 19:6, 2 Peter 2:5,9.) Although we live under a different covenant than the Old Testament priests, the priestly role is similar.[1] Deuteronomy 21:5 explains:

Then the priests, the sons of Levi, shall come near, for the LORD your God has chosen them to serve Him and to bless in the name of the LORD; and every dispute and every assault shall be settled by them.

On many occasions the Lord instructed the priests to come near to God and be His representatives to the people. The priests were also chosen to carry the Ark of the Covenant, which contained God's laws and was accompanied by His presence (Deuteronomy 10:1-8).

In the same way, the Lord wants us to be His representatives on earth. But we don't carry His laws around in a box. He wants to write them on our hearts and fill us with His Spirit. His presence will then emanate from us, bringing love, healing, and blessing to all those with whom we come in contact.

God didn't want priests to simply perform religious rituals. He wanted the heart of each one to beat to the rhythm of heaven, and his own ears to hear God's loving intent for His people.

But first the priest's own heart must be cleansed, his own sacrifices prepared (Leviticus 2:11). There could be no yeast in the grain offering—no pride to cause him to be puffed up with his own self-righteousness. He had to be able to identify with the people. The priest's hands and feet had to be washed as he gazed into the bronze basin made from mirrors (Exodus 30:19). He had to see himself for who he was, and how desperately he also needed God's grace! To accurately represent the King, a priest's life needed to be marked by humility.

WHAT'S CAUSING THAT SWELLING?

At a conference years ago I heard James Ryle make this statement:

> "Pride is disagreement with God. For example, if God were to say to you, 'You are scum of the earth,' pride would say, 'that's not true, how can you say that about me?!' Humility would say, 'I am scum of the earth.' Conversely, if God were to say, 'you are king of the earth,' pride would say, 'Oh, you must be thinking of someone else!' Humility would say, 'I am king of the earth.' Pride is disagreement with God."

The words stunned me! I was familiar with a more classical definition of negative pride: to have an excessively high opinion of oneself, often accompanied with the belief that one is superior to others. I certainly didn't think I was superior to God, but now I had a different understanding. Any time I think I know more than He does—for instance, when I continue to worry when God says to trust Him, or when I think my sins or the sins of others are too great to be forgiven—I have entered into pride. I have elevated my opinions over God's, and am in disagreement with what He says to be true.

So, with a heavy weight of conviction I asked the Lord to show me where I was in disagreement with him. Was I ever shocked! He said I didn't approve of His leadership choices. I didn't agree with His timing or methods, and much more! Overwhelmed with grief I entered into a time of repentance.

1 Peter 5:5 says that *"God is opposed to the proud, but gives grace to the humble."* Verses 8-9 say that the devil *"prowls around like a roaring lion, seeking someone to devour."* But we can *"resist him, firm in faith."* The word "resist" is the Greek word "anthistemi,"

which means to stand against or oppose. This is very similar to the word "antihistamine."

When a foreign substance enters your body through your pores, airways, digestive system or blood stream, there may be an allergic reaction. Your immune system may not recognize the substance due to misinterpretation or incomplete information it receives. As a result, histamines that can cause irritation or swelling are released to fight off the presumed invader. Antihistamines counter these allergic reactions and can even stop them before they take place.

One Friday night after a busy week at work my husband and I went out for a nice seafood buffet dinner at a resort a half-hour drive from our home. It was refreshing to relax with a lovely dinner in the warm, delightful atmosphere, and let the cares of the world slowly dissipate.

When we got home though, Doug started to itch uncontrollably. We took a look and noticed big red welts on his body. No wonder he itched! It didn't take long to figure out he was having an allergic reaction to his seafood! So I ran down to the drugstore and bought some antihistamines. Thankfully, in a short amount of time the itching stopped, and the welts disappeared.

Just as there is something out of order in our physical body that causes allergies, there is something out of order within us that triggers pride — our sinful flesh which wants to rule. When we've been hurt or our rightness on an issue has been challenged, it's easy for us to take an attitude of superiority toward the one who hurt us. We may mouth the words of forgiveness, but our heart remains unchanged. We may think we are more righteous and deserving of God's grace. But God only gives grace to the humble.

The enemy encourages our flesh to swell up with pride by demanding justice, misinterpreting events or encouraging us to operate with incomplete information. He lies about God's goodness and faithfulness so we will be in opposition to God, misrepresent Him, and be in agreement with the devil! But we can resist (anthistemi) Satan by moving in the opposite spirit — humbling ourselves before

God and others! We have to face the truth that there's only One who is right. He alone can bring justice, accurately interpret situations or give us needed information if and when He so chooses. I love what my friend said, "He's God. You're fired!"

His silence does not mean He doesn't care. He's working a much larger plan than we can possibly grasp that will fill us with wonder and delight when it's finally revealed. The King of Kings and Lord of Lords is utterly, entirely good, and He has chosen to make us the object of His outrageous affection. We don't have to prove anything!

Also, we don't have to think less of ourselves because we have been wounded. We may get hurt, but those hurts or the things we've lost can't keep us from being who God created us to be. We don't have to beat on ourselves because of our weaknesses, or deny our gifts and abilities. We can thank God for our strengths and weaknesses, and believe that He will finish what He started in us (Philippians 1:6). When humility is evidenced, He loves to hang around, and His very presence enables us to fully enter into our destiny in Him.

His presence is similar to grease in the bearings of a wheel that enables it to move smoothly and effortlessly in a forward direction with minimal corrosion or friction to wear it out. The thickened oil allows the wheel to do what it was created to do. If we rely on our own strength or ingenuity without God's presence we may have some functionality because of our God-given design, but at some point we will come to a grinding halt. When we humbly grasp God's grace, we have new freedom and courage. One moment we can be on our face acknowledging our sin, and the next we can boldly enter His presence, even as the prophet Isaiah experienced in the following story:

A KING AND A PROPHET

The fame of Uzziah, the great king of Israel, spread abroad for his skill and innovation in equipping his soldiers for effective warfare.

But with his strength came pride.

Uzziah entered the temple and burned incense before the altar of the Lord — a duty that was reserved for the Levites.

Blinded by his pride, he thought his success, popularity, and blessing made it unnecessary to adhere to God's ordained process. When confronted with his sin, Uzziah became enraged.

Immediately leprosy broke out on his forehead — the outward covering of his mind, the seat of his own logic and reasoning that caused him to defy God.

He was quickly ushered out of the temple, and remained separated from God and the people for the rest of his life (See 2 Chronicles 26.)

In the year that king Uzziah died, Isaiah saw the Lord sitting on a throne, lofty and exalted, with the train of His robe filling the temple. He heard the seraphim cry out, *"Holy, holy, holy, is the Lord of hosts, the whole earth is full of His glory."* He felt the foundations of the doorposts tremble at the sound of the voice calling out, and the temple filled with smoke.

Isaiah fell on his face and cried out, *"Woe is me, for I am ruined! Because I am a man of unclean lips, And I live among a people of unclean lips; For my eyes have seen the King, the LORD of hosts."*

When he saw the King, the awareness of his own sinfulness was devastating! But a seraphim came and put a burning coal upon his lips and said, *"Your iniquity is taken away and your sin is forgiven."*

Then Isaiah heard the King speak. *"Whom shall I send, and who will go for us?"*

The once terrified Isaiah boldly stood in the presence of the LORD, the righteous, yet merciful One, and cried out, *"Here am I, Lord, send me!"* (See Isaiah 6:1-8.)

I can imagine him waving his raised hand and shouting with joyful anticipation, "Pick me, pick me!"

Isaiah got it. Yes, he saw his own sin, but he didn't stay stuck there. When he received God's forgiveness, he could then forgive himself and step into his destiny.

Isaiah went to God many times on behalf of the people and stood before kings declaring the word of the Lord. He faithfully recorded all the things God told him, even though he often faced rejection, because many of his prophecies would not come to pass for hundreds or thousands of years.

But he was humble. He had nothing to prove, he knew who God called him to be, and God's empowering presence and outrageous love sustained him.

Without humility our forgiveness of others will be shallow and we will continue to suffer torment. But He invites us to come near. He wants us to behold Him in all His glory and experience His grace. As we do, His presence will prepare us to stand as priests before God on behalf of others.

> *But we all, with unveiled face,*
> *beholding as in a mirror the glory of the Lord,*
> *are being transformed into the same image from glory to glory,*
> *just as from the Lord, the Spirit.* —2 Corinthians 3:18

PAUSE & PONDER...

1. Earlier we quoted Mark 11:25-26, "...*if you do not forgive, neither will your Father in heaven forgive your transgressions.*" If you have chosen to forgive, it may be that God wants to take you into a deeper level of receiving His forgiveness. Can you ask God this same question, "Lord, where am I in disagreement with you?" Jot down what you hear.

2. Do you need an "anthistemi"? If God revealed some areas of pride, agree with God's assessment, ask Him to forgive, and receive His grace.

3. James Ryle defines humility and grace this way[1]:

   "**Humility** is the God-given self-assurance that eliminates the need to prove who you are and the rightness of what you do. It's the freedom to be who God created you to be and to do what God called you to do. And it is the attitude that yields to it because it's God and it's right."

"**Grace** is the empowering presence of God enabling me to be all who God created me to be and do what He has called me to do."

Ask the Lord to show you what these definitions mean for you personally.

4. Thank God for His kindness that leads us to repentance (see Romans 2:4) Again, be profuse. Thanksgiving gives you access into His presence (Psalm 100:4). Give thanks until your whole being feels thankful, and you feel His presence.

---

[1] The Aaronic priesthood, direct descendants of the High Priest Aaron, offered sacrifices *on behalf* of the people, and provided the animals, wine, grain, etc. The Levitical priesthood offered sacrifices *of* the people, who gave the priests the animals, wine, grain, oil, etc. Yeshua (Hebrew name for Jesus) was neither, but rather of the priesthood of Melchizedek, a priest forever (Hebrews 7:3). However, He fulfilled both the Aaronic and Levitical Priesthoods. He provided Himself on behalf of the people, and submitted Himself to the priests of that day so that they could hand Him over to be crucified.

Corruption came into the Aaronic and Levitical priesthoods because of sin and intermarriage, but Jesus was the perfect sinless high priest, whose body did not see corruption, because He was raised from the dead on the third day before this could occur. Both the Aaronic and Levitical Priesthoods had to make their sacrifices on a regular basis, year in, year out, generation after generation, in the *hope* that God would be pleased with them all. Yeshua's once and for all sacrifice never *needed* to be or *could* be offered again. His sacrifice pleased God, or rather *satisfied* God's requirement for justice. That is why it was once and for all! (Information provided by Michael Cohen.) For more on Melchizedek priesthood see Genesis 14:8; Psalm 110:4; Hebrews 5: 6,10; 6:20; 7:1-27.

[2] James Ryle, www.truthworks.org, *Living a Legacy*, Part 4, The Splendor of Grace

❧ 15 ❧
Seasoned with Salt

After a priest's own cleansing, he made the appropriate sacrifices on behalf of the people. Not only were the grain offerings to be free from yeast, as we discussed in the previous chapter, they also were to have something added:

> *Season all your grain offerings with salt. Do not leave the salt of the covenant of your God out of your grain offerings…*
> — Leviticus 2:13

Salt is very durable, acts as a preservative, adds flavor, and is necessary for life. In early times salt was so valued it was used as a form of money. In fact, we get the term "salary" from the word salt.

When people made a covenant with one another, they sealed the agreement with a meal together that had been seasoned with salt to indicate the enduring nature of their commitment. They were not just entering into a legal agreement; they were purposely choosing friendship with each other, and if necessary would defend each other. Salt, even to this day is a sign of friendship and loyalty. In fact, a common saying in the Mideast is, "There is salt between us."

Adding salt to the grain offering was a symbol of an everlasting covenant between God and the Children of Israel. But it was also the heart of the Father crying out for friendship with His people, whom the priest represented, "Come, and let us have a meal together. I will be your God. You will be My people; what is Mine is yours, your family will be My family, and My family yours."

YOU ARE SALT IN THE WORLD

While walking by the Sea of Galilee Jesus spoke to some fishermen, "Follow Me, and I will make you fishers of men."

Amazingly, they did! If you were to ask them why, it would have probably been difficult to put into words. There was just something about Him—the authority with which He spoke, the joy in His smile, the love in His eyes... How can you explain it? They were compelled.

When Jesus saw crowds gathering, He went up on the mountain and sat down. Soon the new disciples were sitting at His feet, so He began to teach. He had so much to tell them in His short time on earth. A new kingdom is here. Jubilee is here. There's good news for the poor, for those who mourn, and those who are captive. Righteousness is available. Lives and communities can be changed and rebuilt (See Isaiah 61). As the crowds pressed in, His voice rose so all could hear.

> *Blessed are the poor in spirit, for theirs is the kingdom of heaven.*
> *Blessed are those who mourn, for they shall be comforted.*
> *Blessed are the gentle, for they shall inherit the earth.*
> *Blessed are those who hunger and thirst for righteousness, for they shall be satisfied.*
> *Blessed are the merciful, for they shall receive mercy.*
> *Blessed are the pure in heart, for they shall see God.*
> *Blessed are the peacemakers, for they shall be called sons of God."*
> —Matthew 5:3-9

The words of Jesus had such power, a sense of pronouncement, as though this man was pledging covenant with them.

"If you mourn I will comfort you...

If you hunger and thirst I will fill you...

If you bring peace into any difficult place, you will be called a son of the Most High God..."

"Blessed" here means "happy and fortunate." Happiness is not in happenings or right conditions. Happiness is found in discovering who God is for us in every situation.

He continued:

> *Blessed are those who have been persecuted for the sake of righteousness, for theirs is the kingdom of heaven. Blessed are*

you when people insult you and persecute you, and falsely say all kinds of evil against you because of Me. Rejoice and be glad, for your reward in heaven is great; for in the same way they persecuted the prophets who were before you."

— Matthew 5:10-12

Then He talks about salt.

You are the salt of the earth; but if the salt has become tasteless, how can it be made salty again? It is no longer good for anything, except to be thrown out and trampled under foot by men. — Matthew 5:13

Is He starting a new thought, or continuing?

Just maybe Jesus was saying, "Guys, listen. This is really important! If you enter into covenant with Me, there will be a cost. My enemy will become your enemy. People will offend you. Some will persecute you unjustly. You must let it go. It's not just about you, others have experienced it before you. But I will share what is Mine with you. All the love, grace, and peace you will ever need can be accessed now, not just in the life hereafter. The atmosphere of heaven can come to earth in the middle of any difficult situation."

"Even as the priests and Levites were to be distributed through all the tribes of Israel (Numbers 35:2-8; Joshua 14:1-5), you are to be scattered like salt in the world:

- A seasoning, preservative, and sustainer of life
- A stimulant that awakens the senses to *"taste and see that the Lord is good"* (Psalm 34:8)
- An active force that stands between heaven and hell crying out on behalf of those the devil would try to destroy
- An agent of change that is ever aiding and assisting society to operate in a healthy, life-giving way
- A symbol of covenant, extending to the world friendship with God.

"But, if you allow offense to take root in your heart, you will become inert and useless to the advancement of My kingdom. If you choose to remain a victim, a victim you will be — trampled on by men, a self-fulfilling prophecy."

A BUSH OR A TREE

Priests were meant to be in community with each other and with those they served. When we go through a great deal of pain, we often don't want anything to do with those who have hurt us, and we are tempted to isolate from others. Let me make this clear: I know some relationships cannot be restored until repentance has taken place and behavioral changes are made. But we are never to harden our hearts. I do not advocate going back into a destructive environment. However, we often don't believe in the power of God to restore relationships, and are afraid to take any risks.[1]

After some of the painful things I experienced it was easy to isolate from others. On a trip back east to see my daughter who was in college, I entered the Baltimore airport feeling desperately alone, even questioning whether God cared. The airport was very crowded with people pressing against one another as they quickly moved toward their destination gates. Then I heard a voice calling above the crowds, "Marilyn! Marilyn! Is that you?"

I quickly glanced around to see where the voice was coming from and saw Ted Roberts, my pastor from Oregon moving through the throng toward me. He was on his way home from Pennsylvania, and I was on my way to Washington D.C. Although it was a very brief encounter it was a tremendous blessing to me. If we had tried to find each other in the sea of people it would probably have been impossible, but God connected us for a brief moment in time. A quick "hello," and we were both on our way again, but I no longer felt alone. God knew right where I was, and He did care. He showed it by connecting me with another person from God's covenant family who knew some of my failure, hurt and pain and still accepted me. Secure in God's love, I could press on and keep walking.

Many times in His life Jesus walked from the Galilee region to the city of Jerusalem for the special feasts where priests and people from every tribe and nation came to worship God, offer their sacrifices, and celebrate together.

Just a few miles east of Jerusalem there is a dramatic climate change. The waters of the Jordan River run into the Dead Sea. Because the sea has no outlet, salt leached from the mountains and earth as the waters make their way downward is deposited in it. The salt content is so high that nothing can survive in it. Even the surrounding area is so salty that little can grow in that desert land. It's fit for nothing but to be trampled upon.

Jeremiah 17:5-6 says the man who does not trust God:

...will be like a bush in the desert and will not see when prosperity comes, but will live in stony wastes in the wilderness, a land of salt without inhabitant.

Let me paraphrase for this specific focus:

If you refuse to trust God, and withdraw from others, you will be like a bush in the salty wastelands that will have just enough life-giving force to sustain it, but will not see prosperity when it comes. And it will come. But you will be so blinded by your fear of getting hurt again that you will not recognize or enter into it.

There will be a series of broken relationships, as people pass through your life, because you choose to remain in that desert place. The sad thing is you will think you are experiencing life, but nothing like what the Lord desires to give you.

But, if you trust God and risk again, you "*...will be like a tree planted by the water, that extends its roots by a stream and will not fear when the heat comes; but its leaves will be green, and it will not be anxious in a year of drought nor cease to yield fruit*" (Jeremiah 17:8). Instead of being merely a survivor, you will be free from fear, and have abundant fruit from your life to share with others.

TAKE A WALK

Have you isolated yourself from others? You may need to take a walk, it's not that far. Can you press past your fear and choose to trust again? God invites you to come to the party. You may need to reconnect with God's people. It's not about the size or style of group or congregation, it's about being children of the King, a covenant people, people of salt, who have come through fire together. Such a people will be loyal, defend, love and serve one another, and extend grace when we fail. And we will fail! We will step on one another's toes as we walk in close proximity to one another. But we have a God who heals and restores.

Then as a company of priests, together we will fight for the preservation of our brothers and sisters in the world who do not yet know God as their Father as we are salt among them.

In this world you will have tribulation and persecution. Consider yourself blessed!

"...*Have salt in yourselves, and be at peace with one another*" (Mark 9: 50). Rejoice and be glad, because great is your reward in heaven.

PAUSE & PONDER...

1. As we stated, the heart of the Father cries out for friendship with His people, whom the priest represented, "Come, and let us have a meal together. I will be your God. You will be My people; what is mine is yours, your family will be My family, and My family yours.'" How would you feel if the person who hurt you was sitting at the table?

   Ask the Lord how He would feel if that person were there.

2. Are there areas in your life where you have disconnected from people?

If so, ask the Lord how He would like you to reconnect.

3. Ask the Lord how He would like you to be salt in your world. What would it look like in your everyday life to be:

- A seasoning, preservative, and sustainer of life.
- A stimulant that awakens the senses to *"taste and see that the Lord is good"* (Psalm 34:8).
- An active force that stands between heaven and hell crying out on behalf of those the devil would try to destroy.
- An agent of change that is ever aiding and assisting society to operate in a healthy, life-giving way.
- A symbol of covenant, extending to the world friendship with God. (See #1 above, "Come, and let us have a meal together, I will be Your God...")

---

[1] If your safety or the safety of children is a concern, seek godly counsel before taking any risks that could be potentially harmful.

❧ 16 ❧
A Healing Community

The promise of Jubilee is that relationships can be restored, families reunited, and prisoners brought home again.

On a bright, sunny day in May our tour bus pulled up to the chalky-white lime rock quarry on Robben Island off the coast of Cape Town, South Africa. It was here that former President Nelson Mandela worked for many of his twenty-six years as a political prisoner during the days of apartheid.

I was deeply impacted by what our tour guide shared with us. This quarry became a university for those who worked there. The men who came from diverse tribes and cultures spent long hours seeking to know and understand one another, rather than let their differences divide them. They had one thing in common. They all wanted freedom for themselves and their people.

These men came to the conclusion that they were not to wait for freedom; they were to prepare for it. So with calloused hands, sweaty, pain-filled bodies, and eyes damaged by the blazing sun reflected on white rock, the doctors, lawyers, teachers, and journalists among them taught others what they knew. For instance, a mathematician drew numbers and theories on the sand while working alongside his "students."

For many years these courageous men had to do their learning in secrecy, but eventually they were given the right to study. Many of these men received degrees while imprisoned, and later became esteemed leaders in the nation.

What could have been a place of bitterness and hatred became a healing community where lives were actually enriched and prepared to set a nation free. We, like the men of Robben Island, don't wait for freedom either. We don't wait for other people to change. We prepare for it.

WE SEEK TO UNDERSTAND EACH OTHER

God has called us to be priests unto Him as part of a healing community. It is here we seek to understand why people are the way they are, the trauma they've experienced and the resulting reactions. We learn to be honest with one another with no fear of judgment, and help each other get free from the inner chains that bind us.

Maybe the one who didn't give you the love you needed never experienced love himself. The one who hurt you may be unable to perceive the pain she's caused.

Several years ago I read an article about two children in England who had no ability to sense pain.[1] The parents filed for disability so they could stay home with them, because they were in constant danger of seriously hurting themselves. For instance, the children would place their hands on the burners of the stove and not feel any pain but receive horrible burns.

One day, one of the parents found the older boy jumping up and down on the stomach of his little sister. They both were giggling and having great fun, but had no concept that this could seriously damage the little girl. They also hurt others, but didn't understand why their actions were inappropriate.

Some people are so damaged by life that they don't understand the pain their actions cause. In a healing environment we can seek to understand why they are so damaged, and then speak the truth in love to help them heal.

Others are locked in their own prisons and can't get out, similar to a bear I read about in a newspaper many years ago.

A zoo purchased the bear from a one-man circus. The owner, who was very cruel, kept him in a cage most of the time, frequently beat him, and only let him out to perform his tricks. Inside the cage, the bear, whose spirit had been broken by the years of harsh treatment, would pace five steps one direction, throw his head back, and thrust his front paws in the other direction, go five steps, and repeat the process, over and over again all day long.

The zookeepers were anxious to give this bear a better place to live, so they fixed up a nice open area with trees, water, and plenty of room to roam. There was a lot of excitement on the day they released him into his new habitat. However, instead of enjoying the new freedom to move about, the bear paced five steps in one direction, threw his head back, and thrust his front paws in the other direction, went five steps, and repeated the process, over and over again all day, all week, all month long. The zookeepers finally realized that although the bear was no longer in the cage, the cage was in him. They eventually put him to sleep.

Sometimes it's easier to have compassion for that bear than for people locked in their own inner prisons. Outward appearances can be deceiving. People can look really together on the outside and function successfully in the eyes of the world, but still be locked in prisons on the inside.

WE FIND A SAFE PLACE TO DEAL WITH OUR SECRETS

During my years of singleness, I led a great group of young college and career singles. One night we sat around together listening to the Lord and giving encouraging words to one another. As I turned to one young lady, I heard in my spirit a cacophony of voices singing, "Secrets, secrets, na na na na na na." Then it was repeated. I gently told the girl what I heard and asked her if it meant anything to her.

Big tears rolled down her cheeks as she hesitantly asked if she could talk to me some time because she was being tormented by secrets from the past. Later she did come and we were able to bring the secrets into the light and find healing for her.

I had a secret, too. I had been molested as a girl, but kept it quiet for many years. I heard someone suggest we invite Jesus into our painful memories and see where He was at the time. Although I felt apprehensive about it, one day I did. I prayed, "Lord, I am thankful that You never leave me nor forsake me. Where were You when that happened to me?" Then I felt a sense of panic, "I don't see You, Jesus, where are You? I feel so helpless!" Fear of going to that painful place tempted me to abort the process, but I persevered. Although I had received healing in the past, I had never been able to reconcile in my mind where Jesus was when this happened. Someone said He was standing there watching. This caused a violent reaction within me. What was He, a voyeur taking perverse pleasure in what He saw? Or was He helplessly standing by unable to intervene?

"Where are You, Lord?!"

Then I heard Him gently speak, "Keep your eyes on Me. Let's go to the cross. I already suffered the injustice. I took this sinful act upon Myself. No one can take your purity from you. I declare you pure and clean. '...It's *what comes out of the mouth that makes a person unclean*' (Matthew 15:11 GW). Bless Me, and forgive once again. He cannot steal from you. You belong to Me!"

I did as the Lord instructed. Then I could see Jesus dressed in pure white, between the man and I, His arms stretched out, protecting me, like a gossamer shield of light. Wave after wave of comfort and love flowed over me.

After a little while I responded, "I am hidden in Christ!" But then my logical mind queried, "Lord, is this an unhealthy escape?"

"No, it happened to your body, but your spirit can live in Me. I put a wall of protection up against pollution."

Amazing revelation! I was not polluted! Christ was the filter! No longer did I feel the need to cry "Unclean!" as the lepers of old. The shame was gone! This was not about forgiveness, I had forgiven long ago. This was about changing my memory of the event. No longer did I look upon it as a place of shame and torment, but God's grace and mercy. I can still see Jesus there, arms outstretched protecting, loving me.

Yet forgiveness was more complete. Now I could truly bless the person who offended me with no reservations!

Since then I have walked with many men and women into those places of secrecy and pain. As we ask, "Lord, where were You?" The Lord reveals Himself differently in each case, but the result is always the same. A place of devastation and wasteland is turned into a well-watered garden. Broken walls are repaired, and ruins rebuilt. Lives and many times relationships are restored.

That's the power of a healing community. There we are able to invite God into all the secret and painful areas of our lives. We learn that He will never leave us or forsake us, and we learn to trust in His mercy and grace.

NEW RELATIONSHIPS ARE FORMED

One night a friend and I decided to go out and have some fun while our husbands were in a meeting. We both had a difficult day and needed a break. Now, our idea of fun may be different than yours. We love to ask God where He wants us to go and what He wants us to do when we get there. This particular night we felt it was Starbuck's. But I sensed in my spirit it was in a different direction than the two with which I was familiar. In my mind's eye I saw us going northeast instead of south or west. My friend said there was a new Starbuck's out that direction.

So we set out on our little adventure.

"Now what do you want us to do, Lord?"

I saw a couple of gals I recognized seated at a table. I didn't really know them, but was aware that they attend our church.

Sensing they were the reason we were here, we asked if we could join them. They gladly said yes, so we sat and talked about the goodness of the Lord, and what He was doing in our lives.

Then one of the gals mentioned a teaching I gave at church some time ago when I shared how my former husband would come home late and I would try to imagine what had happened, but there was murder in my heart (story shared in Chapter 6). In my message I mentioned that I knew some of them had entertained similar thoughts. Then I talked about the importance of what we think. Thoughts determine actions, actions determine ways, and ways determine our final destination. Thoughts are like seeds. If you only think about your lack, that's all you'll have. But if you think about the goodness and faithfulness of God, you will harvest a crop of provision from the Lord.

My new friend told me how those words had encouraged her, because she could relate. We laughed about the commonality of our thoughts. At the same time, there were unspoken words that identified us as understanding some of where the other person had been. We took responsibility for our thoughts, but said nothing evil of those who had caused the pain. We talked about strawberry cake, sweet potato pie, and the best place to get BBQ ribs.

They felt honored that we would spend time with them. And we felt honored that we could get to know these precious women, so loved by God. The waitress eventually told us the store was closed and they were ready to go home. So we stepped out into the parking lot on a busy street, took hands and prayed. I don't know what other people looking on thought about these four women holding hands in a circle, two black and two white. But for me, I thought, "This is church! This is FUN!"

WE LEARN TO MINISTER UNTO HIM

I am passionate about worship unto the Lord. I love to spend time in His presence, sing and play songs to Him in private, and worship together with others. However, worship is much more than singing songs or mouthing words of praise. Jesus said when we feed the poor, clothe the naked, and visit widows and prisoners *"...to the extent that you did it to one of these brothers of Mine, even the least of them, you did it to me"* (Matthew 25:34-40).

Who are the least of them? *Barnes Notes on the New Testament* describes the least as, "One of the obscurest, the least known, the poorest, the most despised and afflicted."[3]

Notice that Jesus didn't qualify why they were in prison or why they were despised. There are some other things He didn't say. He didn't say to keep them from receiving consequences for their actions. He didn't say to try and gain their approval. Our approval comes from God alone. He didn't say to provide for them for life or get them out of prison. He said give them a meal, a drink, visit them, be hospitable. Clothe those whose nakedness has been revealed to you through the wounds they've caused. Don't cut off your heart of compassion.

Will everyone change? Will all relationships be restored? No. There are some people who will never love or approve of us no matter how hard we try. That realization can cause immense grief and pain in us. Our love or efforts to gain their approval are not enough, and they are unwilling to receive God's love. But our hearts will be changed.

We get to choose the attitudes with which we will approach them. They may not be relationally safe, and boundaries may need to be in place, but our hearts toward them can be soft and pliable in the Lord's hands.

When the priests served the Lord in the tabernacle, they were able to see by the illumination of the candlestick. God wants to give us the light of revelation to see with His eyes "the least of these," the "obscurest, the least known, the poorest, the most despised and afflicted." In serving them, we serve Him, and He receives it as worship.

Jesus said in John 12:26, *"If anyone serves Me, he must follow Me; and where I am, there My servant will be also; if anyone serves Me, the Father will honor him."* That's an amazing concept. If we are in an intimate relationship with Him, hear His heart, and follow Him, we don't have to worry about direction—where to go or what to do. We are going to be where Jesus is. We may meet with Him in the heavenly realms through worship and intercession, or with a group of friends. He may then lead us to a penthouse or a slum.

"Jesus is the water of life. Water flows downhill. If we would be where Jesus is, then we must seek Him where He is always going—to the lowest point—of suffering, hurt, fear, death and shame."[4]

God is calling us to be a community where all can be changed, healed and set free.

ᴔ◆ᴔ

PAUSE & PONDER...

1. One of the names for Jesus is Emmanuel, "God with us." He entered into our world to bring salvation to us. Ask the Lord to help you enter into the world of the one who hurt you. What is God's perspective?

   a. Is this person more like the children with no pain sensors or the bear? Why?

   b. Ask the Lord to fill you with His compassion for this person.

2. Are there areas of pain or remaining scars that Jesus has yet to deal with in your life? If so, invite Jesus into those places. Ask Him to show you His presence there. What do you see? Hear? Allow Him to embrace and heal you. Journal what you experience.

3. Who would you consider "the least of these" in your life?

   a. Ask God to show you how He sees them.

   b. Is there a practical way He would have you serve them?

4. Ask the Lord how you can help make your home, group, church, or community a healing place.

---

[1] This rare genetic disorder, Congenital Insensitivity to Pain with Anhidrosis (CIPA), makes people unable to feel pain, heat, and cold. <http://www.answers.com/topic/cipa>

[2] Albert Barnes, Robert Frew, Ed., *Barnes' Notes on the New Testament*, E-Sword Bible Software

[3] John and Paula Sandford, *Healing the Wounded Spirit*, (Victory House Publishers, 1985), 410

~ 17 ~
Chosen to Bless

While at the Robben Island quarry our guide told us that one young man was assigned the job of hauling the rock from one location to another. He had no truck but a simple wheel barrow to carry out the back-breaking work. One of the older men spoke words of encouragement to him, "One day you will be Minister of Transportation!"

And one day he was!

In biblical terms, the older man blessed the younger. He created a reality of what was possible for the young man that inspired him to see beyond his present circumstances, dream, and become more than he otherwise would have been.

One of the duties of the priests was to *"bless in the Name of the Lord"* (Deuteronomy 21:5). The word bless in Hebrew is *barak*, which means "to kneel" or "praise."[1] The first time the word is used is in Genesis 1:22, *"God blessed them, saying, 'Be fruitful and multiply, and fill the waters in the seas, and let birds multiply on the earth.'"*

Blessings came from the greater to the lesser (Hebrews 7:7) — fathers to children, leaders to people, and from God to us. The one being blessed would take a position of humility, normally kneeling before the one blessing. Remember, God counts greatness differently than we do. Jesus said that *"...whoever wishes to become great among you shall be your servant..."* (Matthew 20:26-28). So, both take a position of humility. Jesus left His position in heaven, and humbled Himself to come to us. We in turn must humble ourselves to receive blessing from Him.

But here is something interesting: *Barak* can also mean to "curse." In Job 1:9-11 Satan tells God that He has blessed [*barak*] Job, but if God removes the blessing, Job will curse [*barak*] Him. In essence Satan said that Job would try to take a prideful position of authority over God, even as Satan did before he fell from his exalted position in heaven. Then the words of Job's mouth would come out as curses instead of blessings.

Job's wife picked up on this demonic thought when she said to him, *"...Do you still hold fast your integrity?* **Curse** [barak] *God and die!"* (Job 2:9).

Proverbs 18:21 tells us that *"death and life are in the power of the tongue."* We were blessed in the beginning to reproduce. We get to choose whether our words will contain the humble seeds of life that reproduce after their kind, or prideful words that kill and destroy.

When God blessed He always spoke a new reality into existence. His words were creative, honoring and life-giving. They contained a promise and His empowering presence and provision to bring them to pass.

Every time Balaam tried to curse the Children of Israel blessing came out of his mouth instead. When the king of Moab tried to get him to override the blessing with a curse, Balaam responded:

> *God is not a man, that He should lie, Nor a son of man, that He should repent; Has He said, and will He not do it? Or has He spoken, and will He not make it good? Behold, I have received a command to bless; When He has blessed, then I cannot revoke it.* —Numbers 23:19-20

Notice the sequence:

- God told Balaam to bless, and gave him the words to say.
- Balaam spoke the words.
- Then God made the blessing an irrevocable reality.

From ancient days it was a time-honored tradition for Hebrew fathers to bless their children, speaking creative, honoring, life-giving words over them. They knew their words were irrevocable. For instance, when Isaac blessed Jacob through the latter's trickery, he could not take it back. It was as though all of heaven was called to attention while the words were spoken, and forces were then dispatched to make them a reality. (See Genesis 27:1-35.)

This form of blessing may be difficult to comprehend because in our family of origin and culture we have not experienced it.

IN SEARCH OF A BLESSING

A few years ago a friend caught me after a meeting at church and said, "I have something for you." I recognized the title of the little book she handed me, because three other people had recommended it around the same time: *The Prayer of Jabez*, by Bruce Wilkinson.[2]

The awesome little book, which has sold millions of copies, is the story of a man from 1 Chronicles 4:9,10 NIV who dared to pray: *"Oh, that You would bless me indeed, and enlarge my territory, that Your hand would be with me, and that You would keep me from evil."*

I read it, and the next morning during worship at our church staff meeting I prayed, "Lord, bless me." As we sang, I remembered a month before feeling an urgency to go see my father who was in the hospital for what was expected to be a brief stay.

Several months earlier I mentioned to my dad that it would be a real gift to his children if he could take a few moments and write out a blessing for us.

In their book, *The Blessing*[3], based on patriarchal blessings in the Old Testament, Gary Smalley and John Trent describe five basic parts of a family blessing:

1. Meaningful touch
2. A spoken message
3. Attaching high value to the one being blessed
4. Picturing a special future for the one being blessed
5. An active commitment to fulfill the blessing.

Now, my father never read *The Blessing*, but I hoped he would be able to put a few nice words on paper. I didn't question whether he loved me. I knew he did although he had difficulty expressing it. Due to an earlier stroke, his short-term memory was not good, so he may not even have remembered my request.

As I drove toward Idaho, I imagined myself taking hold of my father's hand, putting it on my head, and saying, "Dad, pray a blessing over me!"

I stopped just over the border in Washington to spend the night at my sister's. She and I planned to go the rest of the way together the next morning. Shortly after we went to bed though, we received a call that our father had died. He enjoyed a good day, visited with family members until they left for the evening, went to sleep, and just stopped breathing.

After we got the news, I lay awake for a long time feeling alone, disappointed, and honestly, a little angry that I didn't arrive in time. Later I found out my dad had a dream in the morning that he was going to die that day. When I heard that, my mind replayed all the possible scenarios, "If I had known I would have left work earlier. I would have..." But I didn't, and there was nothing I could do to change that fact. No blessing.

As we sang in that staff meeting, I envisioned myself taking Father God's hand, placing it on my head and saying, "Bless me, Father. Bless me."

It's a great prayer to pray, except I realized it was coming from a sense that I had to beg. I didn't really believe that God *wanted* to bless me. Intellectually I knew He did, but my heart was not fully convinced.

My mind went to Jacob when he wrestled with the Angel of the Lord and said, "*I will not let you go unless you bless me*" (Genesis 32:26). Jacob struggled to receive a blessing, first from his father, who favored his brother over him, and then from his uncle Laban, who changed his wages repeatedly. Now Jacob was desperate for a blessing from the Lord. Yet, if you look, it's easy to see that God's hand of blessing was on him even before he was born, although his own father did not recognize it.

I, like Jacob, thought I had to overcome God's reluctance to bless me. A subtle shift came into my thinking that day as I again prayed, "Lord, bless me." This time there was a new awareness in my spirit that I didn't have to overcome God's reluctance; it was His desire and *delight* to bless me. In fact, He has!

Then the Lord spoke something I had often heard, *"I have loved you with an everlasting love...before I formed you in the womb I knew you..."* (Jeremiah 31:3; 1:5). He has given me meaningful touches on many occasions. He has given me awesome promises concerning my future. He has committed Himself to bringing them to pass. He has blessed me!

He has blessed you too.

We often equate blessing with a trouble-free life, but the Lord says in John 16:33 *"In the world you have tribulation, but take courage; I have overcome the world."* Troubles will not keep God's blessings from coming to you! He loves to show Himself strong in difficult situations, *"Wait 'til you see how I'm going to bring you into greater blessing through this one!"*

God told Abraham:

> *...I will make you a great nation, And I will bless you, And make your name great; And so you shall be a blessing; And I will bless those who bless you, And the one who curses you I will curse. And in you all the families of the earth will be blessed.* — Genesis 12:2,3

In Deuteronomy 28:1-13 God delineates these blessings to the Children of Israel (Abraham's descendants) if they will obey His commands. You could summarize these blessings as:

- Honor
- Health
- Fruitfulness
- Success
- Provision
- Victory
- Favor with God and man

The Apostle Paul said that Christ redeemed us from the curse of the Law, so that we might receive the same promises given to the descendants of Abraham (Galatians 3:13-14,29). We can walk in these blessings if we abide in Jesus, and He will also show us how to be a fountain of blessing for others as well.

"Father, bless them, too!"

PAUSE & PONDER...

1. How easy is it for you to comprehend the concept of blessing? How is God's idea of blessing different from ours?

2. Have you ever felt like you had to overcome God's reluctance to bless you?

3. Meditate on the blessings from Deuteronomy 28:1-13. Ask the Lord to show you which one/ones He wants you to focus on. One may immediately stand out to you, or your eyes may be drawn to a particular one through a subtle impression. Once you've decided, ask the Lord for revelation on how He wants to bless you in that area. Sit quietly and listen, then write down what you hear.

    You will be blessed wherever you go (vs. 6). *"The LORD your God will bless you in the land He is giving you"* (vs. 8). *"You will be blessed in your towns and in the country"* (vs. 3).

    You will be blessed in everything you do (vs. 8). *"The LORD will send rain at the proper time from His rich treasury in the heavens to bless all the work you do"* (vs. 12).

    You will be blessed in your relationship with God and others. [He] *"will establish you as His holy people as He swore He would do"* (vs. 9). (Note: holiness is lived out in our relationships with people.)

    You will be blessed with fruitfulness. *"Your children and your crops will be blessed"* (vs. 4). You will be blessed *"with many children and productive fields, fertile herds and flocks"* (vs. 11).

You will be blessed with provision for today and tomorrow. You will be blessed with baskets overflowing with fruit, and with kneading bowls filled with bread, an abundance of good things (see vs. 5,11). *"The Lord will guarantee a blessing on everything you do and will fill your storehouses with grain..."* (vs. 8).

You will be blessed in warfare. *"The LORD will conquer your enemies when they attack you. They will attack you from one direction, but they will scatter from you in seven"* (vs. 7).

You will be blessed with authority and honor. *"...The LORD will make you the head and not the tail, and you will always be on top and never at the bottom"* (vs.13).

You will be a blessing in the nations. God will exalt you above all the nations of the world (vs. 1). *"...You will lend to many nations, but you will never need to borrow from them"* (vs. 12). *"...All the nations of the world will see that you are a people claimed by the LORD, and will stand in awe of you"* (vs. 10).[4]

4. Now spend some time thanking Him for His promises.

---

[1] Strong's #1288.
[2] Bruce Wilkinson, *The Prayer of Jabez* (Multnomah Publishers, 2000)
[3] Gary Smalley and John Trent, *The Blessing* (Samas Nelson, Inc., 1986)
[4] Scripture quotations are taken from the Holy Bible, New Living Translation, copyright 1996, 2004. Used by permission of Tyndale House Publishers, Inc., Wheaton, Illinois 60189. All rights reserved.

~ 18 ~
X Marks the Spot

The Lord instructed Moses to tell Aaron and his sons (the priestly line) to bless the sons of Israel saying:

> *The LORD bless you, and keep you;*
> *The LORD make His face shine on you, And be gracious to you;*
> *The LORD lift up His countenance on you,*
> *And give you peace.* – Numbers 6:24-26

You might paraphrase it this way:

> The Lord honor you with His creative promises and provision,
> and put His hedge of protection around you
> so everything He has spoken will come to pass;
> The light of the Lord's presence shine upon you,
> bringing revelation of His thoughts and ways
> as you learn to live in His favor;
> The Lord lift His smile of approval upon you,
> and give you health, prosperity, and peace.[1]

Then something interesting follows. The Lord said when the priests blessed the people, *"So they shall put My name on the children of Israel, and I will bless them"* (vs. 27 NKJV).

I love this! It's like God is saying, "When you speak this blessing over them, you will mark them with an X indicating 'blessings go here,' and I will do it! You speak the words that I give you, and I'll back them up with My presence and provision to bring them to pass."

One day when I was pastor-on-call at our church, a young man came in to see me. His wife had recently left him and he was having a difficult time at work. He felt hurt and rejected, and was fighting bitterness. I gave him counsel and helped him in the forgiveness process. Then I got an idea. I gave him a blank piece of paper and a pencil and told him to ask God any question he wanted, and then draw whatever picture came to his mind. The idea had to come from God because in the natural I "knew" that this was too open-ended, but I decided to trust this impression.

He said, "I want to ask Him about my future."

Inwardly, I lifted my favorite prayer at times like this, "Oh, God, oh God, oh God!"

My mind argued, "As if God is going to show him his whole future!"

But I said, "Great. Now just focus on the Lord and see what comes."

I had a little nudge in my spirit that I needed to do the same thing for him. Immediately the verse from Psalm 1:3 came to mind, *"He will be like a tree firmly planted by streams of living water…"*

So, I hid my paper from him and drew a tree with a little bird on one of the limbs, and a stream with little fish jumping up to indicate life.

When he was done we compared our papers. He drew a tree, some ducks, and a semi-circle abutting the top of the page. I asked him what the circle was and he said, "A pond."

I eagerly exclaimed, "Do you see that! We drew the same thing!"

He responded, "No, you have fish and I have ducks."

"But don't you see? I only drew fish because they indicated life. We each had a tree, water, and life. God is saying to you that your future will be full of life!"

He sat there for a moment as tears came to his eyes. Then wiping the tears he said with emotion, "I didn't think I had a life." I knew the chance of us drawing the same thing was minimal. It was a supernatural gift from God to show this young man that he did have a bright future ahead of him.

I love what Graham Cooke says:

"When people have been damaged, it is the future that can release them from the past. The present is merely rerunning memory tapes and is therefore more prone to repeating scenarios from the past. The future alone calls people up to a new beginning."[2]

When we understand that God's blessings, His words of promise and provision in our lives, cancel out any of the curses of others, new hope rises within us. Then we find it much easier to keep the commands of Jesus, *"Bless those who curse you, pray for those who mistreat you"* (Luke 6:28).

Paul, who endured torture and betrayal, put this into practice, *"...when we are reviled, we bless; when we are persecuted, we endure* (1 Corinthians 4:12)."

IT IS TIME TO BLESS

So if we deal with our mind and emotions by stepping into the role of priest, how do we do that? How do we bless?

Leviticus Chapter 9 gives us insight into this. Aaron lifted up his hands toward the people and blessed them. Then he offered the sacrifices that contained the three things that we mentioned earlier: the lamb, the grain, and the wine.

These three things are all symbolic of Christ and His work on the cross. With each an exchange is made. We bring the earthly, the natural. He gives in return the heavenly, the supernatural.

The Lamb represents:
- Covering for sin – *"The next day* [John the Baptist] *saw Jesus coming to him and said, "Behold, the Lamb of God who takes away the sin of the world"* (John 1:29). Jesus was the Passover Lamb slain for each individual family, but He also fulfilled the sacrifice on the Day of Atonement (Yom Kippur) for the sin of us all.[3]
- Redemption – *"For you know that it was not with perishable things such as silver or gold that you were redeemed from the empty way of life handed down to you from your forefathers, but with the precious blood of Christ, a lamb without blemish or defect"* (1 Peter 1:18-19).

- Restoration of righteousness – *"Though your sins…are red like crimson, they will be like wool"* (Isaiah 1:18).

Sometimes it's helpful to use your God-given imagination as you're learning to bless. Your imagination is not evil, as some think. What we choose to imagine determines whether it is good or evil. This is not meant to be a formula, but an example of how you could pray.

Imagine yourself putting a white covering on the person who has offended you. For clarity, we will continue to call him Sam. (Any of you Sams out there, don't take it personally!) Then pray something like this, inserting the appropriate name or pronoun:

"Father, again I ask you to forgive <u>Sam's</u> sin. Cover <u>him</u>. Thank you that Christ paid the debt for <u>his</u> sins, even if <u>he</u> has not yet repented. Your word says that while we were yet sinners Christ died for us. You have provided forgiveness for <u>him</u>. I ask you to do on earth those things that are available in heaven. May <u>his</u> sins that are like scarlet, be as white as wool. I bless <u>him</u> with the ability to behold and enter into relationship with Jesus, the Lamb that takes away the sins of the world."

Pause, and let that sink in before moving on to the next one.

The grain represents:
- The broken body of Jesus – *"And when He had taken some bread and given thanks, He broke it and gave it to them, saying, This is My body which is given for you; do this in remembrance of Me'"* (Luke 22:19). Jesus was crucified not only at the time when the lambs were being slaughtered (Passover), but also the time when the sickle was being put to the grain.
- Provision – *"I am the bread of life; he who comes to Me will not hunger…"* (John 6:35).

- The Word of God – *"Man shall not live by bread alone, but on every word that proceeds out of the mouth of God"* (Matthew 4:4).
- Healing – *"and He Himself bore our sins in His body on the cross, so that we might die to sin and live to righteousness; for by His wounds you were healed"* (1Peter 2:24).

Imagine yourself now putting a loaf of bread in Sam's hands.

"Father, I ask you to make <u>Sam</u> hungry for Your Son Jesus-- the Bread of Life, the Living Word, whose body was broken so <u>he</u> could be healed and restored to You. Set <u>Sam</u> free from the lies <u>he</u>'s believed about Your goodness and faithfulness. Bring Your truth to <u>him</u>. I bless <u>him</u> with the ability to enter into relationship with You as <u>his</u> Father, experience Your presence, and receive Your words that will take root and grow and produce an abundant harvest of blessing in <u>his</u> life and the lives of all <u>he</u> touches."

Again, pause. You may want to read it again.

The wine represents:
- The blood of Jesus – Before the crucifixion, Jesus gave the cup of wine to His disciples and said, *"this is My blood of the covenant, which is poured out for many for forgiveness of sins"* (Matthew 26:28).
- Life for a life – *"For the life of the flesh is in the blood, and I have given it to you on the altar to make atonement for your souls…"* (Leviticus 17:11). The lifeblood of the lamb was given in exchange for the life of the person who sinned.
- Joy – The Feast of Tabernacles was a wonderful time of rejoicing over sins forgiven and the abundant harvest God had given them. *"He causes the grass to grow for the cattle, And vegetation for the labor of man, So that he may bring forth food from the earth, and wine which makes man's*

heart glad, So that he may make his face glisten with oil, And food which sustains man's heart" (Psalm 104:14-15). Jesus turned water into wine in Cana, which was a very joyous occasion.

- The Holy Spirit — The disciples on the day of Pentecost were accused of being drunk with wine when the Spirit was poured out upon them. The Apostle Paul said, *"Do not get drunk with wine...but be filled with the Spirit"* (Ephesians 5:18). Life, joy, freedom, forgiveness, and relationship that the wine symbolizes are accessed through the Holy Spirit.

Now imagine yourself placing in Sam's hands a bottle of wine (or grape juice, if you're more comfortable with that).

"Thank you, Father, for the blood of Jesus which was poured out for <u>Sam</u>. You gave Your life in exchange for <u>his</u>. Your Word says that no one can come to You unless the Spirit draws him. Draw <u>Sam</u> unto Yourself. Send Your Holy Spirit to bring conviction. It's Your kindness that will lead <u>him</u> to repentance. I ask you to fill all the hurting, wounded places in <u>his</u> heart that would cause <u>him</u> to hurt others. May <u>he</u> experience Your love in a way <u>he</u> never has before. I bless <u>him</u> with the joy that comes from knowing You." (See John 6:44, Romans 2:4)

Then bless the way you would want to be blessed, with the same extravagance that you would like to receive. Ask the Lord if there are more ways He would like to bless this person. How does the Lord want to reveal Himself in his life? What is the future the Lord desires for him? Then declare these things as blessings.

I know the words may be difficult at first, but remember, Jesus never asks us to do something He will not give us the power to do. You may never have known how much this person needed Jesus if he hadn't offended you. When you step into the role of priest and bless, you get to partner with God to help bring the offender into right relationship with Him and become a blessing instead of a curse to the world. A wonderful side benefit is you also set yourself in a position to receive more blessing from God!

What if the person is already dead? Bless him in your memory. Since the events are still living and active in your mind, I would encourage you to imagine yourself standing before the person and blessing him as described previously. You may not be able to change his personal history, but you can change your attitudes toward him. Bless any descendants, and ask the Lord to heal any wounds or judgments they may have received as a result of his actions. Thank the Lord for the ways you have learned to trust in Him as a result of what you experienced.

"SAFE FORGIVENESS"

"You saved my life," the beautiful woman before me said. We were eating lunch together after four days of teaching in a seminar overseas.

"Huh? What do you mean?"

"When you shared on forgiveness I got a horrible headache[4]. I didn't feel like going back the next day, but knew I must." Then she proceeded to tell us her story. She had been victimized by someone who caused her a great deal of pain and shame. She had given, as a friend of mine calls it, "safe forgiveness" — just enough forgiveness to feel like she was alright in her relationship with the Lord, but not enough to be free. Bill Johnson expresses it this way, "Many Christians repent enough to get forgiven but not enough to see the kingdom."[5] We come out of Egypt, but stop short of entering into the land of promise.

In her thoughts she always referred to him as "that man." It was as though he were a non-person with no facial features. The words "I forgive you," were a way to release him from her mind, but did nothing to release him from her heart. Finally, she heard the Lord tell her she must call the man by name. She wrestled with the Lord for a time until finally she blurted out, "I forgive you, _____," and she said the man's name. Immediately, she saw his face in her mind, and relived all the things she had tried so hard to bury. But this time something was different. This time there was a release in her spirit and peace as she blessed this man who had tormented her thoughts for so long.

TWO YOUNG GIRLS

While teaching in South Korea, I asked a group of students at a missionary training school to sit and listen to the voice of God. The question I asked was, "Father, what is one of your thoughts about me?" based on Psalm 139:17-18, "*How precious also are Your thoughts to me, O God! How vast is the sum of them! If I should count them, they would outnumber the sand...*"

After the meeting, two young high school girls approached me with the aid of an interpreter. When the first girl did the exercise she heard the word "hatred." I knew something was wrong here, because that is not the nature of my Lord.

"Has anyone hurt you?" I asked.

Yes, teachers and classmates had made fun of her.

"Have you forgiven them?"

"Yes."

"Can you now pray blessing on them?"

I didn't need an interpreter for this. The expression on her face was very clear. She shook her head with an emphatic "NO!"

I realized she heard the word "hatred" because God was lovingly pointing out what was in her heart—hatred toward herself and others. Then as gently as I could, I said that she hadn't yet fully forgiven. I explained more what it means to forgive, and the joy of blessing those who persecute you.

Then I asked if she could now pray blessing on them, "Bless them the way you want to be blessed." She prayed an awesome prayer that they would come to know Jesus and that God would bless them.

Afterwards I asked her if she was ready to listen to God again.

"Yes," so she bowed her head and listened for a few seconds. Then she raised her head and smiled.

"What did you hear?" I asked.

"He said, 'Thank you for forgiving.'" Her countenance and demeanor totally changed.

The other friend had been listening. Her body language was also one of rejection, and self-loathing. Obviously, she too had experienced much pain over the rejection of others. I said, "You've heard what we've talked about. Are you ready to pray blessing also?"

She nodded. So I said, "Go ahead and do that." She also prayed a wonderful prayer of blessing. Then I had her listen again to the Lord. She radiated, "He said He needs me!"

These delicate young flowers were transformed from victims to partners with God in bringing redemption to the earth. Their desire was to be used by God on the mission field. They just learned a great lesson on how to reach others through the power of forgiveness and blessing!

WHAT WOULD YOU LIKE TO RECEIVE?

"Can you bless them?" I asked the man sitting before me at a prayer counseling session. Joe was working through some forgiveness issues with some people who had hurt him deeply. He said he could and began to pray around the issue, but he just couldn't quite get the words of blessing out of his mouth.

Finally, I said, "Joe, can you bless them the way you would like to be blessed? What would you like to have? Ask God to give them the same thing."

He thought for a moment, and then said, "Well I want peace and rest. So, Lord, I pray that you will bless them with peace and rest."

Then an amazing thing happened. It was as though a light bulb came on in his head, as God revealed to him a profound truth, "Oh, I get it now! When I judge others I actually send them unrest. Then because I am judged in the same way I judge, I also receive unrest!"

His countenance changed, and Joe was able to bless them freely with a heart of compassion. God revealed by His Spirit in a moment's time what words could not do.

JUST SAY "NO"

There's one final thing. **Stop rehearsing the past.** Don't keep replaying the hurtful event over and over in your mind. Let it go. There are some things you will never understand or be able to fix. But God is still faithful. He's bigger than the pain of the past.

One day I stood at my kitchen sink doing dishes when I heard this pitiful voice playing in my head, "Ohhhhh, if they only knew what I've been through. (Sigh.)"

I was startled! What is THAT?! I was having a good day, no bad thoughts about anything, but I realized that I had entertained that voice for so long, that now a demonic presence was attached to it. As has been said, "Self-pity is Satan's favorite babysitter."

I quickly repented to the Lord for listening to that voice. No more! The enemy overplayed his hand!

When your mind starts to wander down those familiar trails, just say "NO!"

As you aggressively bless others eventually your mind and emotions will line up. You will enter into a new place of rest and peace in the Lord.

Then look in the mirror. You will see that you're looking more like your Father everyday!

To sum up, all of you be harmonious, sympathetic,
brotherly, kindhearted, and humble in spirit; not returning evil
for evil or insult for insult, but giving a blessing instead;
for you were called for the very purpose
that you might inherit a blessing.
– 1 Peter 3:8-9

PAUSE & PONDER...

1. Read again the section on the lamb, the grain, and the wine above. If you have not yet done so, I encourage you to pray the prayers over each person you forgave earlier. For a complete list of the 5 R's of Forgiveness, see back of book.

2. Ask the Lord how He wants to additionally bless the person(s). What is the future that God desires to give him/her?

3. Form a prayer of blessing incorporating what the Lord speaks to you. Put on a card or in a prayer notebook, and pray on a daily basis. Remember, bless as you would like the Lord to bless you, so put your heart and soul into it. That may be difficult at first, but as you begin speaking the words and set your will to bless, your heart will eventually engage!

---

[1] Peace is the Hebrew word shalom which comes from the verb leshelem ("to pay" or "make complete"). It includes health, prosperity, and peace. (Strong's #7965)

[2] Graham Cooke, *Approaching the Heart of Prophecy* (Punch Press, 2006), 115

[3] When Jesus died on Passover He somehow also had to fulfill the Yom Kippur requirement as well. How did He do that? By the first words He spoke from the cross, "Father forgive them, for they do not know what the are doing." Passover and Yom Kippur both required the death of an animal, one to be consumed (Passover) and one to be burned (Yom Kippur)—one to be offered by every family (Passover) and one to be offered ONLY by the High Priest (Yom Kippur). Jesus (Yeshua) perfectly covered these as well. His death was not only for the Jews, but "When the Son of Man is lifted up, I will draw ALL MEN to me." He was our Great High Priest, and His sacrifice occurred once for all men.

[4] Physical manifestations can often occur when there is demonic oppression, which often accompanies bitterness.

[4] Bill Johnson, *Face to Face with God* (Charisma House, 2007), 59

≈ 19 ≈
Don't Miss Your Appointment!

When I was four and a half, my family welcomed my baby sister into our home. Disposable diapers were only a dream in those days, but diaper liners at least helped. To this day I remember the chest of drawers where my mom kept them. Frequently I would go into that room, open the bottom drawer, and breathe deeply of their delicate fragrance.

It's amazing that even today when I catch a similar scent I can quickly be transported back to that time and place!

The lamb, grain and wine that the priests offered as sacrifices were a pleasing aroma unto the Lord (Exodus 29:41). It was as though He would stoop low to the earth and breathe deeply from the scent of the fire rising before Him. Perhaps He was transported to another time centuries before.

When Noah and his family left the ark he built an altar and offered a sacrifice. When the Lord smelled the soothing aroma, He promised He would never again destroy every living thing (Genesis 8:20-22). We may be shocked at the way people treat one another, but God is not. Yet He still graciously looks for a reason to bless us. When He smells the aroma of a heart fully surrendered to Him, willing to bless instead of curse, He remembers His promise.

Sometimes, though, blessing with words is not enough. More may be required of us.

OUTCAST

"I can't believe this is happening!" Anya thought to herself. A friend of hers had given some hurtful admonitions to ministry leaders in a conference meeting, and people assumed that Anya agreed because she was standing with her. But she was as shocked as everyone else!

A few days before the conference, her husband said, "Anya, I don't want you to go to the conference, but I know you must."

"I know. My spirit is uneasy about it too."

It was difficult to put into words. Apprehension. Dread. So, not knowing what it was all about, she fasted and prayed for three days before she went. Then at the pre-meeting prayer on the first night she had a vision. The Apostle John in long robes and white beard walked among the people with sadness in His eyes saying, "Little children, love one another."

Things were beginning to make sense now. The dread and apprehension she felt beforehand were a warning that something was going to happen. but she never imagined the unfolding of events to come. People took sides over what was said in the meeting; some agreed, and others violently opposed. Her friend was repentant for the way the message came across and wanted to make things right as best as she could, but the damage was done.

About a week later Anya tried to talk with Sophie, the conference organizer, about the incident but was soundly rejected with anger and bitter words. Sophie blamed Anya for what happened and warned people to stay away from her. As a result, there were accusations and much gossip about her in the Christian organization where they both worked. Anya felt like an outcast, and didn't know what to do.

Jesus was the ultimate sacrifice that brought a pleasing aroma unto the Lord. If we have died to earthly things and our life is now hidden with Christ in God, that aroma is also on us. To those looking for truth, the sweet aroma of Christ in us compels them to come closer to the Source. (See Ephesians 5:20, Colossians 3:2,3, 2 Corinthians 2: 15-16). But honestly, sometimes it's difficult to stay dead and hidden in Christ. We come alive with thoughts of retribution, judgment, or self-justification. Another aroma can easily emerge!

Although it was increasingly difficult for Anya to be on staff in the same organization, she felt she was not supposed to leave her position. But in prayer one day the Lord revealed to her that she had taken on an unpleasant aroma—some attitudes toward leadership because of the rejection she felt. She also said some things in private out of her frustration and pain that were not honoring to them.

"Lord, what should I do?"

"Repent."

So she went to the ministry leaders and asked forgiveness. Anya felt freer than she had in months, but she still didn't know how to deal with Sophie. Every time thoughts came she prayed blessing on her, but nothing changed.

Then Anya had a dream. Sophie was at the top of an escalator and couldn't come down. The only thing Anya could do was go up to her. "Lord, how do you want me to do that?"

A gift. So Anya decided on one and went to her and said, "Sophie, I'm sorry we haven't been able to resolve this issue between us. I again ask you to forgive me for anything I have done to hurt you. I make a pledge to you today that, no matter what, I will choose to love you. What you do is up to you."

Sophie thanked Anya for the gift, but basically said she couldn't make the same commitment. But it no longer mattered to Anya. She had done what God asked her to do. Now it was in His hands.

Then an interesting thing happened. Many people went quietly to leadership about Sophie's increasing negative behavior. When Sophie was confronted, anger escalated, and she eventually left the organization with many of her followers.

A few told Anya they were sorry for gossiping about her, but at that time there was no acknowledgement from leadership.[1] Fall turned into winter, and winter into spring, then summer, and fall, and life went on.

THE GLORY APPEARS

God promised Noah the seasons would always remain, *"While the earth remains, seedtime and harvest, and cold and heat, and summer and winter, and day and night shall not cease"* (Genesis 8:22).

We may think seasons come and go and nothing has changed, and resolution may not come the way we hoped, but God is still behind the scenes working things out for our good. Recently, I did a scriptural study on the word "season." I discovered that season is also translated as an appointed time, place, sign, or meeting.[2] It is the same word as "meeting" in the phrase "tent of meeting," where Moses and the priests met with God.

God has set on His calendar some appointments that, if we choose to bless others, we will not miss! But we have to keep showing up at the tent of meeting, our place of daily appointments with the Lord, where we experience intimate friendship with Him, and are continually cleansed, anointed, and prepared to bless the people and stand before God on their behalf.

After making the proper offerings, Moses and Aaron went into the tent of meeting:

> ...**When they came out and blessed the people, the glory of the LORD appeared to all the people.** *Then fire came out from before the LORD and consumed the burnt offering...and when all the people saw it, they shouted and fell on their faces.*
> –Leviticus 9:22-24

That would have been an awesome sight, wouldn't it?

What is glory? The Hebrew word kabod means glory, honor, splendor, dignity, reputation, and abundance. It comes from the root word *kabad*, which means weighty.[3]

As you stand in the role of the priest and bless, you can be a vessel through which the weighty revelation of God's glory, splendor, dignity, reputation and abundance is revealed to others. It's as though scales fall from the eyes to reveal the beauty and majesty of who He really is.

AN APPOINTMENT WITH A CITY IN PAIN

"I need to share on forgiveness at some point," I told my teammate on a trip to Northern Ireland. We were in a city where a major bombing had taken place during the height of the IRA conflict.

"Sure, wherever you feel it works in best," Kathy told me.

At each meeting I checked in my spirit, "Is now the time?"

Friday night, "No."

Saturday morning, "No."

Then in the afternoon session I felt a release to share. I briefly talked about forgiveness and the need to bless. The people sat with stony expressions on their faces, and I knew I had touched a raw nerve. They all had either lost family or friends, or knew someone who did.

Then a barrage of questions came, "How can you forgive when they haven't repented?"

"Remember, forgiving doesn't make right what the person did. It's simply a matter of letting God be their judge and not you."

"But, how can we bless them? What they did was too horrible!"

"When you bless them, God gets to choose how that blessing will come. He is still a just God. But what better blessing could there be than for them to turn from their sins and come to know Jesus?"

Then a man in the back spoke up, reflectively, as revelation came to him. "You know, there was one man who was thrown into prison for what he did. He was stripped of everything, and had nothing in his cell except a Bible. Because he was bored, he started to read it. The more he read, the more he realized his own sinfulness. He repented, and became a Christian."

With excitement I said, "He was blessed, wasn't he? What better blessing could there be!" The whole atmosphere in the room changed as people began to comprehend the power blessing could bring.

We went through a time of forgiveness and blessing, and afterwards a couple who were not present the night before, nor during the morning session came up and shared their own struggle with forgiveness. This was the only meeting they could attend.

This couple and the man in prison both received an appointment on God's calendar.

That whole city had been affected by injustice. But imagine what could happen if a few people allowed the sweet aroma of Jesus to penetrate their clothing as they spent time in the secret place with

Him. What if they stepped into the role of priest, blessed, and asked the Lord to set up appointments with those who in the world's opinion did not deserve it? A whole city could be changed!

God has some very special appointments set up for us also. Paul, in 1 Corinthians 2:9-10 NIV says that:

> ...*No eye has seen, no ear has heard, no mind has conceived what God has prepared for those who love him" but God has revealed it to us by His Spirit...*

He goes on to say that we cannot accept these things without this same Spirit of God that anointed Jesus living and active in us.

God wants to reveal His glory to us in much greater ways. As mentioned earlier, Moses cried out to the Lord and said, *"Show me Your glory!"* and God said, *"I Myself will make all My goodness pass before you"* (Exodus 33:18,19). If the world is ever going to be filled with His glory, then you and I need to let them see the goodness of the Lord through us as we are continually filled with the Spirit of God.

Sometimes, though, we can be the ones who stop the flow of God's glory from being fully released.

AN APPOINTMENT WITH THE HEALER

"You've never heard a man who speaks like this man!"

"Come, I've seen Him do amazing things! He will heal you!"

The news about Jesus was spreading everywhere. People came and were not disappointed.

But Jesus would often slip away to the wilderness and pray. Although He was God, He had chosen to be limited to human flesh. He needed to commune with His Father, and be filled afresh with the Holy Spirit, even as we do today.

One day He was teaching in a home meeting, and the room was filled with Pharisees and teachers of the law who had come from Galilee, Judea, and Jerusalem to hear Him.

The power of the Lord was present for Jesus to heal the sick, but no one could get through to Him because of the crowd.

Some resourceful men would not let the multitude dissuade them. They had a friend who was paralyzed and could not get to Jesus, so they went up on the roof and began to remove tiles. When they had a hole that was big enough, they lowered the man down into the middle of the crowd in front of Jesus.

When Jesus saw their faith, He spoke to the man, "Friend, your sins are forgiven."

The Pharisees and teachers wanted to hear something they could either agree with or somehow disprove. Now their ears were on fire! Of course, they were too proper to speak out loud, but inwardly they were shouting, "Who does He think He is! Only God can forgive sins!"

The faith-filled atmosphere was quickly changing to darkness as their judgmental thoughts spread a putrefying stench through the room. Jesus, aware of what was going on in the spirit realm, confronted them immediately:

> *"Why are you reasoning in your hearts? Which is easier, to say, 'Your sins have been forgiven you,' or to say, 'Get up and walk'? But, so that you may know that the Son of Man has authority on earth to forgive sins," — He said to the paralytic — "I say to you, get up, and pick up your stretcher and go home.'"*
>
> –Luke 5:22-24

He did, glorifying God as he went!

Did you notice? The Spirit of the Lord was present to heal. There was an open heaven through which the glory of the Lord could be revealed, but it could not be accessed because Jesus was surrounded by those who were filled with their own judgments of how the "minister" should speak and act.

There were many on the stage that day—the Teacher, the learners, the observers, the critics, and some men who simply loved their friend. They refused to get sidetracked by their own judgments or bitterness towards those who would not give them access to Jesus, and found the place of the open heaven! They blessed not only with words, but action. They had an appointment to keep with the Living Word, the Healer who put His teachings into practice!

And the glory of the Lord came down when love found a way!

PAUSE & PONDER…

1. Have you ever been in a room where gossip and criticism were going on? How did it make you feel? How would you describe the atmosphere?

2. Have you ever been wounded by leadership?

   Have you tried to resolve it?

   Even though you may feel right about your position on an issue, have you taken on any wrong attitudes? If so, take some time and ask the Lord how He would like you to make it right.

3. Have you ever experienced a time when it felt like the glory of the Lord came down?

   How would you describe *that* atmosphere?

   Was there any transformation in your life that took place?

4. Do you have daily scheduled appointments with the Lord? If not, ask the Lord how and when He would like to meet with you.

---

[1] Although ideally it should have been done at the time, years later the issue was discussed openly with leadership and resolved and wounds began to heal.
[2] *Strong's* #4150
[3] *Strong's* #3519 and 3513

⇜ 20 ⇝
Whose Sin is Greatest?

After my divorce, rumors ran rampant. A few years earlier I felt led of the Lord to share about my own emotional affair in a women's Bible study I was teaching. Although it was difficult, the Spirit of the Lord was present in a powerful way. Several women came and thanked me secretly afterwards. They were either caught in a similar situation or were considering it, and what I shared helped them break free.

But some thought those things should not be spoken in a public setting. It wasn't proper! They didn't speak to me directly about it, but word got back to me through the gossip mill.

Now rumors were flying again. "You better keep your husbands away from her. After all, she once had an affair!" At a time when I needed love the most, many people were cruel—again, most not to my face. The last thing on my mind was having an affair with anyone. There was nothing worth going through that pain again!

Once again I had to forgive, choose to love, bless those who were gossiping against me, and find refuge in the Lord.

Gossip and judgments have a way of sucking the life out of a room, and creating an atmosphere that invites the minions of hell to gather around like wolves, licking their lips as they encircle their prey.

"GO AND SIN NO MORE"

The days in Jerusalem had been long. Jesus had come from Galilee for the Feast of Tabernacles. His brothers tried to persuade Him to come earlier, because they thought He ought to come to Jerusalem to make Himself known. They didn't believe in Him or understand that He wasn't trying to make a name for Himself. This was not His assignment.

Although He was the Son of God, He was also the Son of Man. It was not easy facing rejection from one's own household. He may have felt stabs of pain in His heart, yet He refused to allow bitterness to take root.

But His heart for the people could not be silenced. "Yes, Father, they are so thirsty and dry, I will go." So He came later quietly on His own (See John 7).

The streets were abuzz with news of this man. People pressed against Him. Religious leaders plotted to kill Him.

He stood in the temple and taught. Arguments and reasoning of men created disorder all around.

"How can He teach like this? He's not educated!"

"He's got a demon!"

"No, He's the Messiah!"

"He can't be. The Messiah is to be born in Bethlehem, and this man is from Galilee!"

Jesus could easily have silenced their arguments, but didn't. Those close to Him knew the truth — at least part of the truth they were able to receive. He knew one day soon even they would reject Him. There were those who wanted Him to seize power from the Romans. And the leaders were afraid He might, and thus bring judgment down on all of them.

Confusion abounded. Yet, He remained peaceful in the midst of it all.

"…If anyone is thirsty, let Him come to Me and drink. He who believes in me, as the Scripture said, 'From his innermost being will flow rivers of living water.'" — John 7:37,38

"Truly this man is a prophet!"

"He can't be. No prophet comes from Galilee!

"Kill him!"

Each held firmly to his own view, and the atmosphere was thick with the oppressive darkness of division and disagreement.

Yes, the days were very long.

The people went to their homes or places of lodging, and Jesus spent the night on the Mount of Olives. Tired and thirsty, He longed for a place of peace away from the cacophony of judgmental, accusing voices. He needed to spend time with His Father.

Early in the morning He went again to the temple, and the thirsty ones gathered around Him, so He began to teach.

Then the scribes and Pharisees brought a woman who was caught in the act of adultery and threw her down in the center of the court before Him.

"You say we don't keep the Law of Moses! Well, the law says she should be stoned. What do you say?!" They sneered at Him, trying to find justification to accuse.

He looked at them, then calmly stooped down and began to write on the ground.

As persistent children who want their own way, they asked Him again. This time He straightened up and said, "He who is without sin among you, let him be the first to throw a stone at her." Then He stooped and began to write once again.

His words were like strategically placed arrows in their hearts. No arguments, no defense, no confusion. From the oldest to the youngest, the scribes and Pharisees quietly left the center of the courtyard.

Jesus and the woman alone remained. Then Jesus looked at her and said, "Did anyone condemn you?"

"No one, Lord."

"Neither do I condemn you, go and sin no more."

Go and sin no more. As I said earlier, God is not soft on sin. But whose sin is greatest? The woman caught in adultery, or those who stand by and criticize, blame, and try to keep others from divine appointments with the One who can save them from their sins?

WHO'S FOR DINNER?

The prayer meeting was a highlight of my week. We were a group of young mothers who came together to intercede for whatever God put on our hearts. Those were rich, meaningful times that laid a deep foundation within me.

One week we sat in the living room of our hostess while she took care of a couple of things that had come up with her family. While we waited, several of the women grumbled about their difficulties with husbands, mothers-in-law, or others. I happened to be silent that day. I would love to say I was "more spiritual," but the truth was on many other occasions I had joined in the negative conversations.

When we finally went in to pray we all got on our knees and asked the Lord what was on His heart that day.

After a little bit, my friend Alice said, "The Lord gave me a scripture reference." We were all very eager to see what the Lord had to say to us, so we excitedly looked up the scripture, Ezekiel 5:10.

However, the anticipation quickly fled as we read, "...*fathers will eat their sons...and sons will eat their fathers...*"

A heavy silence fell on the group. We all thought, "Wow, she really missed that one! That couldn't be God!"

Then, with atmosphere tense with awkwardness, we went back to prayer.

Slowly, as my thoughts turned back to God, from out of my spirit another scripture arose:

> "*But if you bite and devour one another, take care that you are not consumed by one another.*" —Galatians 5:15

I caught my breath as I was suddenly filled with the fear of the Lord. God had called us to be priests, crying out on behalf of others; instead we were devouring them with our words! It was unmistakable. He was saying, "How dare you sit and gossip and judge others with your mouths and think you can come into My presence and be heard!"

WE ALL HAVE GRAVE CLOTHES

After Lazarus had been dead four days, his friend Jesus came to his tomb and wept. Jesus delayed coming because He had no intention of healing the sick man. He had a greater purpose the people could not yet understand. Some Jews gathered there said, "See how He loved him." Others were offended, "He opened the eyes of the blind man, couldn't He keep this man from dying?"

Jesus had the stone rolled away and cried out, "Lazarus, come forth!" Then Lazarus emerged from the open tomb bound head to toe in burial wrappings. "Loose him, and let him go," Jesus told those standing nearby. I have often imagined them taking a piece of the cloth and twirling him around like a top! But it was probably a slow, messy job; undoubtedly the stench of death was still upon the burial garments.

Some Pharisees now believed in Jesus, but others ran to tell religious leaders what He had done. They did not rejoice in the miracle of new life, or get involved with the process of releasing Lazarus from his grave clothes. Instead, the gossips and critics talked on.

Then they began to plot the death of Jesus.

❧ ◆ ❧

PAUSE & PONDER...

1. Judgments and gossip work hand in hand to bring us into agreement with the plans of the evil one to destroy the life of Jesus in others. Rather than gossiping about people, Jesus wants us to help release them from their grave clothes.

   Have you ever been the object of gossip? How did it make you feel?

2. The Bible is very clear about God's feelings towards gossip. (See Proverbs 11:13, 16:28, 20:19, 26:20; Romans 1:29-32; 2 Corinthians 12:20; and 1 Timothy 5:13.) Yet it is one sin, we easily excuse in ourselves and others.

   Are there specific people or places that cause you to be vulnerable to gossip?

4. If needed, take a few moments and ask the Lord to forgive you for gossiping about others.

5. Ask the Lord to help you come up with a plan to break that cycle of gossip. Write out that plan and find someone to hold you accountable.

❧ 21 ❧
Fear of the Lord

If anyone had a right to be bitter and judgmental this young man did. He was taken from his country of birth, removed from his family, and made a slave in the house of the king. It didn't stop there; he was probably stripped of his manhood, never to know the love of a woman or rejoice at the birth of his first child.[1]

Yes, he had every right to be bitter. But not Daniel! He did not focus on his hurts or the wrongs he suffered. Instead, he and his three friends centered their attention on God.

It would have been natural to at least wring some good out of their situation. When taken into the king's courts they could have enjoyed the impressive delicacies offered to them. They chose instead to please God, not man—even if that "man" was their own appetites. They would not compromise with the world system into which they were thrown, nor would they become bitter because of the hand dealt them.

They also were never disrespectful toward the authorities they served. They simply took their stand, with full knowledge that they may suffer the consequences of that stand. They walked in a peace that was supernatural, yet readily available to all who will put their trust in the Lord.

When thrown into the fiery furnace because they refused to bow down to a statue of the king, Daniel's three friends said, "Our God is able to deliver us, but even if He doesn't, we will not bow before your gods." You're probably familiar with the story of their miraculous deliverance. A fourth man appeared in the furnace with them, and the three came out with their bondages removed, yet without even a hint of fire or smoke upon them, and the pagan king glorified God (Daniel 3).

Many years later, Daniel also refused to stop praying to the Lord God, and consequently, through the trickery of jealous, evil men, he was thrown into a lion's den. Yet he still did not become bitter. The mouths of the lions were sealed, and another king glorified God (Daniel 6).

When Daniel read the prophecy of Jeremiah that the children of Israel would be in captivity for seventy years, he fasted and prayed. It was time. The years had been ticking away, and the season for the fulfillment of Jeremiah's word was at hand.

Like Elijah on Mt. Carmel, when the Lord told him it was going to rain so he prayed until it came (1 Kings 18:42-46), Daniel knew that the promise would not automatically come to pass. Many times the promises of God require a birthing process.

So Daniel, this man who was righteous and faithful to God, fasted and prayed, identifying with his people. While he was yet speaking and confessing his sins and the sins of his people, the angel Gabriel appeared to him and said, *"O Daniel, I have now come forth to give you insight with understanding. At the beginning of your supplications the command was issued, and I have come to tell you, for you are highly esteemed..."* (Daniel 9:22, 23).

Why was Daniel so highly esteemed? Why did God desire to give him insight and wisdom?

TRIP TO THE LIBRARY

My husband Doug and I were in Hawaii for a much-needed vacation. While on our trip I tried to learn how to do Sudoku puzzles. But it wasn't just the puzzles I was trying to figure out; somehow in my mind I thought if I could just figure out the mathematical equations or patterns of how these work, then some of the other issues in my life would begin to fall into place.

Now, I know this seems irrational. Honestly, if others had come and confessed this to me I would have told them they were trying too hard. "Trust God. Rest in Him. His yoke is easy, and His burden is light" (Matthew 11:30).

The Lord dealt with me differently. He gave me a dream.

In this dream I walked with the Lord into a library. It was not a tremendously impressive one—just a small city library. The Lord said He was making this library available to me. I could read any of the books I wanted. He made it clear that I didn't own the books — they belonged to him — but I had full access.

I awoke with a sense of excitement.

"Lord, what is this library?" I questioned.

The answer quickly came into my spirit, "All the wisdom of the ages is available to you. Just come."

I could hardly wait! "Lord, will you please take me on a tour of this library?"

"Come, daughter, this section is called science."

Inwardly I groaned, "You've got to be kidding! Science was not my best subject!" Feelings of inadequacy intensified! But I said, "Open a book for me, please."

His response was instant, "No, I want you to open one."

Then in my mind I could see a room with books as high and wide as I could see. This was no small library!

Overwhelmed I said, "Lord, where do I begin?!"

The words, *"The fear of the Lord is the beginning of wisdom,"* immediately arose in my spirit (Psalm 111:10).

"Then, Lord, teach me to fear You!"

In the vision in my mind I could now clearly see a book illuminated. On the spine were the words, "The Fear of the Lord." All the other books were still there, but this one had a bright glow around it. The library did not seem as daunting anymore, and a peace settled over me. I knew the fear of the Lord was the key to all the wisdom that I need!

What does it mean to fear the Lord? It means to be so filled with awe, reverence, and wonder at the holiness, power, majesty, and goodness of God, that we worship Him alone and fear nothing else. We fearfully RESPECT His power, we KNOW His character, we BELIEVE His love, and we TRUST His faithfulness to keep His promises.

As I was writing this book, I asked the Lord one morning, "Can we go into Your library again?"

Immediately I heard in my spirit, "Good Works."

"You've got a whole section called 'Good Works'? Let's go!"

I was surprised when I saw only one book. Again, it was labeled, "The Fear of the Lord." Then more books appeared, and I heard the words, "A book of remembrance." I knew this was from Malachi 3:16, but let's read it in context:

> *"You have said harsh things against me," says the LORD. "Yet you ask, 'What have we said against you?' "You have said, 'It is futile to serve God. What did we gain by carrying out His requirements...?"* —Malachi 3:13,14

Sometimes we don't say these things audibly. They may be thoughts in our mind, or attitudes that seep out under pressure. We may have forgiven in the past, but offenses continue to come. When we have been wronged it's easy to think, "Lord, I'm trying to serve you. Look at all I've done! Now I've lost something that can't be regained. I don't have the resources, abilities, or emotional constitution to fulfill Your purpose for me."

We look at our ledger book of good works or favor with God and think we can never measure up. Our account looks like it's in the minus column. Then we again keep a record of wrongs done to us, so that we can somehow be able to explain to the Lord why our account is lacking. Or, we may take offense at God and withdraw from Him.

As we've said before, we will never please God by our good works. But God does want to write a book about us:

> *Then those **who feared the LORD** spoke to one another, and the LORD gave attention and heard it, and a book of remembrance was written before Him for those who fear the LORD and who **esteem** His name.* —Malachi 3:16

The word "esteem" in this verse means to reckon, account, calculate, plan for action, think and consider.[2]

It's the same word used in Genesis 15:6 and Romans 4:3, "*Abraham believed God, and it was __credited__ to him as righteousness.*" It's also used in Philippians 4:8 when Paul tells us "*...whatever is true, whatever* is honorable, whatever is right, whatever is pure, whatever is lovely, whatever is of good repute, if there is any excellence and if anything worthy of praise, dwell on these things." The Amplified says, "think on and weigh and take account of these things [fix your minds on them]."

When we speak to others about God's faithfulness, rather than singing our "Somebody Done Me Wrong" song, when we erase from our ledger (that we can never balance) the names of those who have hurt us, God writes our name in His ledger, and credits us with righteousness. When we esteem — think about, consider, take into account, plan a course of action based on — His name and the good things He has done for us, God gets excited and says, "Angels, write this down! I want to remember this! Listen to what he's saying about Me! Now he's giving Me some material that I can work with to bring blessing and favor upon him!"

HE'S IN MY BOOK

Daniel was highly esteemed because he feared the Lord and highly esteemed His name. Daily he kept his appointments with the Lord whether he experienced favor or was under attack. He planned his course of action based on his love and devotion to the Lord, not on the approval or fear of man. Every time he chose to trust God, instead of getting bitter and resentful, God wrote a new entry in His book of remembrance! And when Daniel prayed, God responded, "I know this guy! He's in My book! Whatever he wants, he can have!"

This man was also highly esteemed by three ungodly kings because of his righteous behavior, and his prayers helped set his people free from captivity!

My friend, there are difficult days coming upon the earth as the distinction between light and darkness becomes more pronounced. More of the glory of God will be revealed, but persecution will also increase as the clash of kingdoms intensifies. As it was in the days of Jesus, the greatest persecution may come from those who think they are doing the work of God. We may be tested by fire or lion's den, even as Daniel and his friends were. Today we get to choose how we will respond in *that* day.

God is looking for those who will fear the Lord and highly esteem His Name. He's looking for those like Daniel who, instead of getting bitter, resentful, and judgmental, will identify with a sinful people and cry out on their behalf.

May God say about us, "Whatever you want, you can have!"

PAUSE & PONDER…

1. Esteem is also the same word used in Jeremiah 29:11, *"For I know the plans that I **have** for you,' declares the LORD, 'plans for welfare and not for calamity to give you a future and a hope."* King James Version says, *"I know the thoughts I **think** toward you."* Personalize this verse by replacing the pronoun YOU with your own name. Then ask the Lord, "What are some of the thoughts You think about me?" Listen, and journal what you hear.

2. To fear the Lord and trust Him, we must know who He is. *"And those who **know Your name** will put their trust in You, For You, O LORD, have not forsaken those who seek You"* (Psalm 9:10).

   Look at some of the names of God listed here. How many of these ways has He shown Himself to you in the past? Be specific. For instance, "When I felt helpless, El Shaddai, the all-sufficient one, helped me in this way…"

   Or, who do you need Him to be for you today?

Names of God

ADONAI — "Lord and Master (Owner)" —Isaiah 6:1
JEHOVAH — LORD Yahweh "The Self-Existent One" —Exodus 3:14
JEHOVAH-JIREH — "The Lord will Provide" —Gen 22:14
JEHOVAH-ROPHE — "The Lord Who Heals" —Exodus 15:26
JEHOVAH-NISSI — "The Lord Our Banner" —Exodus 17:15
JEHOVAH-M'KADDESH — "The Lord Who Sanctifies" —Lev 20:8

JEHOVAH-SHALOM — "The Lord Our Peace" —Judges 6:24
JEHOVAH ELOHIM — "LORD God" —Genesis 1:1
JEHOVAH-TSIDKENU — "The Lord Our Righteousness" —Jer 23:6
JEHOVAH-RO'I — "The Lord Our Shepherd" —Psalm 23:1
JEHOVAH-SHAMMAH — "The Lord is There" —Ezekiel 48:35
JEHOVAH-SABAOTH — "The Lord of Hosts" —Isaiah 6:3
EL ELYON — "Most High" —Genesis 14:19-20
El SHADDAI — "All Sufficient" —Genesis 17:1
EL ELROI — "The God who Sees" —Genesis 16:13
EL OLAM — "The Everlasting God" —Isaiah 40:28
KADOSH — "Holy One" —Isaiah 40:25
YESHA — (Y'shua "Savior") —2 Samuel 22:3
JESUS

3. Daniel identified with the children of Israel when he stood on their behalf and asked God to forgive his sins and theirs, even though he was a righteous man. Ask God if there are any individuals or people groups He would like you to identify with in prayer, even as Daniel did?

---

[1] There is no record that Daniel or his three friends ever married or had offspring. The Lord told Hezekiah in 2 Kings 20:18, "...*some of your descendants, your own flesh and blood, that will be born to you, will be taken away, and they will become eunuchs in the palace of the king of Babylon.*" This could have easily happened to these four young men as well.
[2] *Strong's #2803, chashab*

ঌ 22 ঌ
Season of Grace

The angel Gabriel continued speaking to Daniel:

"Seventy weeks [literally seventy sevens, or seventy times seven] *have been decreed for your people and your holy city, to finish the transgression, to make an end of sin, to make atonement for iniquity, to bring in everlasting righteousness, to seal up vision and prophecy and to anoint the most holy place."*
—Daniel 9:24

Did you pick up on that? There it is again—seventy times seven. The children of Israel had gone into captivity for seventy years because they did not obey God's laws and show mercy to others. Now God said, "I am giving you a season of grace."

My purpose here is not to give my futuristic interpretation of this biblical prophecy. Sometimes we get so intent on figuring out the theology or timing of events in the Bible that we miss seeing the heart of God.

God's dealings with the Children of Israel reveal not only His righteousness and holiness, but also His grace and love. When Peter asked, "How many times shall I forgive," and Jesus responded, "Seventy times seven," I think He was saying two things. First, "If you do not forgive, you will be tormented, even as the Children of Israel were," as we discussed earlier. He also may have been saying, "Peter, the Father has given them a season of grace to end their sin and atone for wickedness. I am the one who has come to pay the penalty for their sins so they can be restored to the Father. Will you extend to them the same grace and mercy the Father has?"

WHO IS SHAKING THE BED?

It is easy for us to slip into casualness with the Lord, where we don't really take His commands to extend grace seriously, as my

169

friend Ruth experienced years ago. When her husband had only been a Christian for about 6-8 months they had a fight, as young couples can easily do. John fell asleep in a contour chair in the family room, and Ruth headed off for bed. The issue had not been resolved, and she was still fuming and grumbling to herself.

Just as she was about to doze off, she felt the bed shake violently. Startled to an alert state, she saw no one was there. Instinctively she knew that it was the Lord shaking the bed. The scripture immediately sprang to mind, *"BE ANGRY, AND yet DO NOT SIN; do not let the sun go down on your anger, and do not give the devil an opportunity. (Ephesians 4:26, 27)."*

She recognized that the Lord was warning her to deal with her attitude immediately before she gave the enemy opportunity to enter an open door in the night hours. With the fear of the Lord upon her, she went into the other room, woke up John, told him she was sorry, and the two made peace between them. Then she was able to go back to sleep in peace, thankful for the Lord's mercy in her life. There's something else to consider, she may have also saved John from opening the door wide to the enemy in his life as well.

We too often cling to our right to be angry, not realizing the effects it can have in the spirit realm.

WHERE'S THE FRUIT?

When John the Baptist was born, his father Zechariah, quoting from Malachi 4:5,6, prophesied that he would:

> *...TURN THE HEARTS OF THE FATHERS BACK TO THE CHILDREN, and the disobedient to the attitude of the righteous, so as to make ready a people prepared for the Lord.* —Luke 1:17

Yes, it is fathers to their children, but you could also say, older to younger, wiser to inexperienced, smarter to less educated, mature to the immature, and so on. It's restoration of relationship. When our attitudes change, when we speak words of blessing, we give others opportunity to bring their attitudes into agreement with righteous thinking, which in turn will prepare them to walk in better relationship with the Lord. They may not take the opportunity. That is between them and God, but it is important that we do our part.

God is looking for the fruit of love in our lives—love for Him and love for others. He has given us a season, but that season is finite. His love never ends, but there comes a time when He allows us to experience the fruit of our own choices.

COUNTDOWN

The years of Jesus' life on earth was now reduced to hours and days. God's time clock was ticking. Prophecy was being fulfilled.

As Jesus approached Bethpage on the Mount of Olives, He sent two of His disciples ahead of Him with instructions to bring Him a colt they would find as they entered the village. "If anyone asks you, 'Why are you untying it?' tell him, 'The Lord needs it.'"

It happened just as He said, fulfilling Zechariah's prophecy centuries before (Zech. 9:9).

As Jesus rode the colt toward the city, spontaneous praise erupted from the crowd who spread their cloaks on the road and shouted, "Blessed is the king who comes in the name of the Lord!"

"Peace in heaven and glory in the highest!"

But the ever-present Pharisees asked Jesus to rebuke them. After all, *reason* and *sensibility* said, "We don't want to stir up the people. We don't want the Romans to think we're trying to set up a king. Although we're in captivity, at least we have some peace. Don't upset it!"

Jesus responded quickly, "If they don't cry out, the rocks will!" If you've ever been in the rocky land of Israel, you know this would be a very loud cry! The season for praising the Lord had come! It was time!

The people shouted for joy. Their king had come! But they had no idea what was soon to take place. Their shouts would soon turn to jeers, their excitement to discouragement.

But Jesus knew. The weight of it was already crushing. When He saw the city of Jerusalem before Him, He wept.

*"If you had known in this day, even you, the things which make for peace! But now they have been hidden from your eyes. For the days will come upon you when your enemies will throw up a barricade against you, and surround you and hem you in on every side, and they will level you to the ground and your children within you, and they will not leave in you one stone upon another, **because you did not recognize the time of your visitation.**"*[1]

—Luke 19:42-44

TIME IS RUNNING OUT

My son-in-law, Dan, was youth pastor at our church for several years. One night at youth group, he felt impressed to talk to the young people about laying their lives down before the Lord, willing to do whatever He asked them to do.

As Dan spoke, he felt the powerful presence of the Holy Spirit, and he kept repeating, "It's time!" "It's time!"

He said an amazing thing happened.

Spontaneously the young people began weeping before the Lord, and some stood up and confessed their sins. Soon on their own they laid down on the floor in a posture of repentance before the large cross in the corner of the room.

It was a very powerful time as the Holy Spirit moved upon the youth.

On his way home Dan asked the Lord about what just happened. He had been in meetings before where there was a lot of emotion, but it was just that—emotion. He knew it wasn't the commitment to the big call of the Lord on their lives, but the daily choices to love God and others that would determine their outcome.

He cried out, "Lord, was that You or not?" The issue weighed heavily on his mind, because he didn't want to just stir up the youth, with no lasting fruit.

My daughter Joy and grandchildren were not in the meeting that night, and knew nothing of what had happened. When Dan arrived home, the children were already asleep.

The next morning Dan took Hannah, the five-year-old, to kindergarten.

On the way she said, "Daddy, I had a dream last night."

"Really, what was it?"

She said, "There was a big cross on the ground, and we all went and laid down on it."

The hair on the back of Dan's neck stood up as he realized God just answered his question from the night before. He mustered a smile, and said to Hannah, "That's silly, why did we do that?"

She responded, "Because there was a great big clock and time was running out."

It is time to turn our hearts toward the Lord and one another, lay down our need to be right, and receive the attitude of the righteous so we don't miss our day of visitation.

❧ ◆ ❧

PAUSE & PONDER...

1. Spiritually speaking, in what areas of your life have you become casual?

2. Meditate on the verse: "...*TURN THE HEARTS OF THE FATHERS BACK TO THE CHILDREN, and the disobedient to the attitude of the righteous, so as to make ready a people prepared for the Lord.*" (Luke 1:17).

   a. Have you lost a sense of urgency in turning people's hearts back to God? If so, why? Do you want to change? Then pray:

      "Father, forgive me for my apathy. Show me how to live with a sense of passion and urgency and adjust my schedule and priorities accordingly. I want to partner with You in helping people discover how good You are."

   b. Ask the Lord specifically who He is preparing to receive Him as King at this time. Your children? Co-workers? Friends? How would He have you turn your heart toward them In prayer? In practical ways?

---

[1] This took place forty years later in 70 AD under the Roman general Titus.

❧ 23 ❦
Final Instructions

In the spring of the year Jesus and the disciples were gathered in an Upper Room (John 13-16). Jews from all over the known world were gathered in Jerusalem to bring their gifts and sacrifices to the temple. Lambs were slain and roasted on the fire, bitter herbs were crushed, bread baked, tables spread, wine poured. The Passover Feast began.

Jesus knowing that He had come from God and was returning to God, got up from the meal, took off His outer clothing, wrapped a towel around His waist, and began to wash the disciples feet.

The greater blessed the lesser. Jesus modeled greatness for them. He humbled Himself and took the role of a servant.

Was there pain in His heart as He lovingly handled the feet of Peter who He knew in a few short hours would deny knowing Him, not once, but three times?

Was there sadness in His eyes as He came to each of the others who would also stand back as though they did not know this man who had walked with them for three years?

Jesus lovingly took the feet of Judas in His hands, knowing He would soon slip out into the night to betray Him for thirty pieces of silver.

What went through His mind?

All the sin of the ages past and the generations to come was about to rest on His shoulders. The weight of it even now was beginning to crush Him. What could He say to these men He had loved so faithfully? What parting words should He give in these important brief moments they had left together?

When He had finished washing their feet, He put on His clothes and returned to His place. Then He asked:

"Do you know what I have done to you? You call Me Teacher and Lord; and you are right, for so I am. If I then, the Lord and the Teacher, washed your feet, you also ought to wash one another's feet. For I gave you an example that you also should do as I did to you." —John 13:12-15

This was not a lesson on cleaning feet. Let me paraphrase for you a little of what He said:

"You call Me Teacher—for three years I have taught you and helped you discover truth, I've modeled life in the kingdom of God before you. I've loved, and in My love, at times corrected you.

You call Me Lord—you have willingly subjected yourself to the authority you see displayed in My life. Now we will find out if I am truly your Teacher and Lord. It must be more than words. Will you love as I have loved, even the one who betrays you?

Oh, the world will soon know the truth of whether I am your Teacher and Lord. They don't care about your words. They will be watching to see if you have love. That's the only thing that will convince them of who I am.

Oh, Peter, you say you will never forsake me. You don't even see the pride in your own heart. But I see, and I love you anyway. I know you can't love on your own. You can only love as you abide in Me, and My words abide in you. The miracles you have seen exhibited before you are released through love. You don't have to do this alone. I'm sending My Spirit to live in you, to empower you to love."

He ate the Passover dinner with them, bringing new meaning to the lamb, the bread, and the wine. Then He went out into the night.

The murderer Barabbas, whose name means "son of the father," was released from his sentence of death as the Son of the Father took his place.

The sacrifice was prepared. The grain offering was salted as sweat streamed from Him in the garden. The Living Bread was broken. The drink offering was poured out as His blood was shed. (See Luke 22: 44,19,20). The innocent Lamb of God hung on a shameful cross. Jesus was a king, but the King of kings and Lord of lords became as "one of the least of these."

> *...He has no stately form or majesty that we should look upon Him, nor appearance that we should be attracted to Him. He was despised and forsaken of men, a man of sorrows and acquainted with grief; and like one from whom men hide their face He was despised, and we did not esteem Him. Surely our griefs He Himself bore, and our sorrows He carried; yet we ourselves esteemed Him stricken, smitten of God, and afflicted. But He was pierced through for our transgressions, He was crushed for our iniquities; the chastening for our well-being fell upon Him, and by His scourging we are healed.*
>
> *All of us like sheep have gone astray, each of us has turned to His own way; but the LORD has caused the iniquity of us all to fall on Him. He was oppressed and He was afflicted, yet He did not open His mouth; like a lamb that is led to slaughter, And like a sheep that is silent before its shearers, so He did not open His mouth.* — Isaiah 53:2-7

All the sins of all people for all time were laid upon Him in the swirling darkness. People jeered, close friends abandoned, and demons cackled as life ebbed from His tortured body.

"My God, My God, why have You forsaken me?!" He agonized from the center cross (Matthew 27:46).

Some other words still haunt me. Unimaginable! How could He?

His plea before the unrepentant crowd, *"Father, forgive them for they don't know what they DO!...Do!...do..."*[1] arose as sweet incense before the Lord, echoing through the corridors of time.

PAUSE & PONDER...

1. Imagine you were present when Jesus washed the feet of His disciples. How does that change your idea of love and sacrifice, knowing that Jesus did this in spite of their unfaithfulness? In what way are you personally impacted by this reality?

2. If we are to love like Jesus we must learn to abide in Him. Do you know what that means? Ask the Lord to give you deeper revelation of how you can abide in Him.

3. Jesus went out into the night to write in blood the story of His great love. Ask Him to write His love on your heart. Sit quietly until you experience His love flowing into you. Then give Him profuse, enthusiastic, heart-felt thanks.

---

[1] Luke 23:34

๛ 24 ๛
Qualified, Not Victimized

My friend, I know I have repeated myself many times and many ways, hitting at this issue of forgiveness and freedom from judgments. I recognize you may still struggle. You may feel like the disciples did that day when Jesus died on the cross. They undoubtedly were tempted with bitterness toward Judas, the government and religious rulers, the fickle crowds, and even themselves for their own failures. Like them, you may feel that your dreams have been dashed, and all hope is gone. You may think no one can really understand. It's true. No one has walked through exactly what you've gone through; many have experienced similar things.

I've shared some of my personal stories. They are forever a part of my history. I have cried bitter tears over things I could have done differently, and rejoiced over the positive changes God has made in me.

I asked my former husband Steve several times if he was okay with my sharing some of our journey. He very graciously said, "Yes, I understand how bitterness toward God and others influenced my decisions. If sharing can help keep someone else from making the same mistakes, it's worth it."

God does not wipe out our memories. But He does bring healing if we let Him.

To me it's like coming across an old picture from the past. Once it was in living, vivid color that you could step into and relive with all its pain and pathos. But when God heals that area, it's as though the picture turns from color to black and white. It's still there. You still remember. But now the word GRACE is written over the top in bold red letters. It no longer holds any pain, fear, or terror, only thankfulness for the wonderful grace and mercy of God.

Repeatedly in the Word we are told to not harden our hearts. Every time we choose to cling to our right to be hurt or get even, to hold grudges, and judge others when confronted with truth, our hearts become a little harder, even as the Pharisees. At some point we have to believe in the power of the gospel to bring healing to us, and choose to walk in it.

My friend Karen received healing in this way. She said that when she tried to forgive:

> "I needed to picture that person on the cross. I needed to see the nails being hammered into the hands, the crown being put on the head, the spear being thrust through the side. I had to yell the taunts, laugh, and scorn. I had to enjoy seeing him suffer. If I'm going to crucify him in my heart, this is what it means. If I want him to suffer and get the full cost of that sin, then this is also what I want for myself. If I have put men in a position that they have to be perfect, then I am saying that I also am required to be perfect. Matthew 7:2 says, *'For in the way you judge, you will be judged; and by your standard of measure, it will be measured to you.'*
>
> What measure do I choose, the perfect man? If so, I've chosen my own crucifixion. But if I choose the measure of mercy, believing that He was the only perfect man, and He took my sin on the cross, then I will also receive mercy. Idolatry can be worshipping a measure or standard. God requires a just balance. The measure I use will be used on me."

God will redeem all your hurt and pain if you will let Him.

LUNCH WITH A FRIEND

About three years after my divorce I spent some time with a new friend. As we shared together over lunch I discovered she had a story very similar to mine. When I drove away from her house, I said, "Lord, even though it's been a while, I still feel some of the pain of what I've gone through. You've healed me so much, but it still hurts." It was like touching a scar and feeling again the pain.

Then something interesting happened. I had my hands on the steering wheel, and it seemed like Jesus was sitting in the seat next to me. Then I heard Him say, as clearly as I have ever heard anything, "Now you know how I feel when my children are unfaithful to me."

I was stunned. Yes, I did know!

I felt His pain, and my heart ached! I wanted to pull off to the side of the road, hold and comfort Him!

I am not a victim! I am an overwhelming conqueror! The Lord shared with me some of His heart. I experienced things that not everyone gets to experience. I am so blessed!

Remember my commitment to God at age fifteen, "Lord, You can do anything You want with my life"? Many times over the years I've said in the midst of pain, "Lord, sign me up again. I haven't changed my mind."

My life prayer has been, *"that I may know Him and the power of His resurrection and the fellowship of His sufferings, being conformed to His death."* Through the things I have experienced my prayer is being answered.

God reveals to each of us different facets of His character and heart. I have come to know God as FAITHFUL. Even though I have been unfaithful, He never has been, nor will He ever be! He's Faithful. That's who He is. *Lord, I want to know You more! If the release of Your power through my life comes through sharing in Your sufferings, then it is worth it! If I must die to my rights that You can live in me, it is worth it! I am not a victim! I am more than a conqueror in you! I am most blessed!*

Not only am I blessed, but I also am in a unique position to bless others.

When Jesus rose from the dead…

Did I mention that?

He really did! Lots of witnesses saw Him. He died on Friday, but rose on Sunday morning. It created quite a stir, you know. At first the disciples didn't believe it. Who would? They saw Him die a horrible death. His lifeless body was laid in a tomb, a large stone was rolled in front of it, and soldiers were placed there to stand guard.

Nevertheless, on Sunday morning He appeared to Mary Magdalene, so she quickly ran to tell the disciples who were hiding in a shut room. (See John 20:18-23.) Later that evening Jesus suddenly appeared before them and showed them His hands and side. He repeated twice, *"Peace be with you!"* It makes sense; after all, they were probably on the verge of a heart attack after His surprise appearance! However, I think it was more than a statement to calm their jittery nerves. He was giving them His peace — the peace He promised (John 14:27). Peace, God's Shalom — the full extent of health, prosperity and peace with God and men.

"As the Father has sent me, I am sending you."

Then He breathed on them and said, *"Receive the Holy Spirit."* The breath of God that was lost in the garden with the fall of man was restored to them. With this life-giving breath Jesus reinstated dominion and authority in the earth, *"If you forgive anyone his sins, they are forgiven; if you do not forgive them, they are not forgiven"* (John 20:23 NIV).

Let me paraphrase:

"I forgave sins and eyes were opened, lame walked, demons were cast out, and the dead were raised. *'As the Father has sent me, I also send you.'* I have demonstrated for you what is possible through a life filled with the Spirit of God. I am sending you as sheep among wolves to do the same things, in fact, greater things (Matthew 10:16; John 14:12). "I am sending you to walk into any situation and bring My peace. Yes, you will have trouble; people will reject you and hurt you. But instead of being affected by their actions, let the peace in you infect them! Forgive sins, as I have forgiven. Speak release to those in captivity."

I don't know if you caught something a few chapters back when Jesus said to the Pharisees:

...Why are you thinking these things in your hearts? Which is easier: to say, 'Your sins are forgiven,' or to say, 'Get up and

walk'? But that you may know that the Son of Man has authority on earth to forgive sins..." He said to the paralyzed man, "I tell you, get up, take your mat and go home."   —Luke 5:22-24

Jesus was the Lamb slain before the foundation of the world (Revelation 13:8). From heaven's perspective it had already happened. He reached into the future that was already established in the past and declared it as a present reality. Notice, Jesus did not forgive as the Son of God, but as "the Son of Man." Jesus said we would do the same things He did. I will say it again: we have the same Holy Spirit living in us that indwelt Christ! The price for sin has already been paid. As priests we can declare it!

Yes, people still have a choice whether they will receive that forgiveness, but we have authority to make declarations in the spirit realm that release the forces of heaven to work in the lives of those enslaved.

One of the principles of the kingdom is that you gain greater authority in those areas where you have personally overcome.

The Lord has led me to walk down the streets of my city and say, "Lord, forgive this one, and that one. Show Your mercy!" Friends and I have asked forgiveness in uninhabited fields or ruins where blood has been shed or violent crimes committed, and declared that the blood of Jesus speaks a better word than the blood crying out for justice.[2] We've then seen those barren places released from the "hell-i-port" from which the devil has operated because of the evil done there, and become developed, productive, and a blessing to others.

We've walked the streets of Jerusalem asking God to forgive the sins of those who continue to reject him—knowing that He has promised to reveal His mercy to them once again. We've bowed on Mt. Carmel in Israel in the middle of a driving rainstorm and set up twelve small stones as a reminder of what Elijah did, when he set up one large stone for each of the tribes of Israel, even though they were divided into the ten tribes of Israel and two tribes of Judah. By this act he declared on earth what was true in heaven—in God's eyes they were still one. We then asked the Lord to forgive the people for all their division and bitterness towards one another, and bring heaven's kingdom to earth in that broken land.

We've walked mountains in North Korea and worshipped the King of kings and Lord of lords, and asked Him to forgive the sins of those who hold the people in bondage through their idolatry and the cunning of men. We've prayed in Germany, Holland, England, Northern Ireland, South Korea....

I've asked God to forgive those who have hurt me, and bless them exceedingly, abundantly, beyond all they could ask, think, or imagine (Ephesians 4:20). I've cried with many people who have sinned against others, and pronounced forgiveness over them. I've seen their lives changed from shame to grace filled, from hardness to the sweet countenance of Jesus upon their faces.

I have not seen the answers to all my prayers, but I know God hears them and the prayers of others as well. I am also confident I have authority in this area because I have learned to forgive. I am not a victim. I am a partner in God's plan to bring His Kingdom to earth.

"Who shall separate us from the love of Christ?
Shall trouble or hardship or persecution or famine or nakedness
or danger or sword?
As it is written: 'For your sake we face death all day long;
we are considered as sheep to be slaughtered.'
No, in all these things we are more than conquerors
through Him who loved us.
For I am convinced that neither death nor life,
neither angels nor demons,
neither the present nor the future, nor any powers,
neither height nor depth, nor anything else in all creation,
will be able to separate us from the love of God
that is in Christ Jesus our Lord. – Romans 8:35-39

PAUSE & PONDER…

1. I mentioned that God reveals to each of us different facets of His character and heart. I have come to know God as FAITHFUL. How has He revealed Himself to you?

2. Through the things you have experienced, how are you uniquely qualified to minister to others?

3. Meditate on the fact that everything Jesus did on earth was as the Son of Man, not the Son of God, and the same Spirit that was in Jesus indwells you. What implications does that have in your life?

   How does it increase your faith?

4. Who needs a spoken word of forgiveness over them today? Your spouse? Your children? A friend, co-worker, or neighbor? Take a risk!

❧ 25 ❧
Peace Enforcers

Although nothing can separate us from God's love, we are engaged in a real battle. The enemy tries to rob our confidence so we cannot take our rightful place of authority before God and the world. He also tries to get us to react in fear to our life circumstances, and then draw us into conflict with others.

God told Moses that when they were going into battle and were greatly outnumbered, a priest was to stand before the army and encourage them to not be fearful (Deuteronomy 20:1-4). As priests, we first enter into peace ourselves, then confront the enemy's lies, and bring peace to those engaged in battle.

Peace is a mighty weapon against the enemy. Romans 16:20 says, *"The God of peace will soon crush Satan underneath your feet..."* Jesus, the Prince of Peace lives in us, so peace is readily available. We are to enforce God's peace on the earth.

SETTLE INTERNAL DISPUTES WITH THE ENEMY

Each of us is assaulted in our minds on a daily basis. Second Corinthians 4:4 says the god of this world has blinded our minds to the truth. There is a difference between facts and truth: the facts say there are more *"chariots and horses and an army that outnumbers yours"* (Deuteronomy 20:1 NIV), but the truth is, *"the LORD your God is going with you, and He will give you victory"* (verse 4). He outnumbers the enemy any day!

We all struggle with unbelief to the degree that we have insecurities, doubt God's abilities, or suspect others. The enemy says we are not good enough, God's not big enough, or people don't care enough. God has given us authority to settle these disputes (See Deuteronomy 21:5).

We speak words of encouragement to people and pray that their eyes will be opened as Elisha did. His servant saw the city surrounded by an army of horses and chariots. When Elisha prayed, though, the servant's eyes were opened and he saw the mountain was full of horses and chariots of fire all around them that far outnumbered the enemy (2 Kings 6:14-17).

When God opens our eyes to see the truth of who He is in any situation, rather than merely the facts from our limited perspective, those internal disputes will be silenced. He sits in the heavens and laughs at His enemies (Psalm 2:4). He invites us to come up and sit and laugh with Him. We can be overwhelmed with His joy instead of by our circumstances.

One time I was praying for one of my children and said to God, "It seems like You are here, and this child is running as fast as possible the other direction." The situation seemed hopeless.

Then I heard God clearly say, "Marilyn, it's okay, the earth is round." This child is going to run right into Him! From the vantage point of heaven I now had reason to rejoice!

We also are to:

SETTLE DISPUTES WITH ONE ANOTHER

God is calling us to a higher place in Him. Romans 12:18 says, *"If possible, so far as it depends on you, be at peace with all men."* People are not our enemy, but we do have an enemy who is constantly trying to bring division between us.

As priests, God's agents of justice, we have authority to plead cases in intercession and do what we can to restore people to Him and one another. We lovingly encourage people to obey the words of Jesus, whether we are the offender or offended.

If someone has offended us, we work through the forgiveness principles explained in this book.[1] If we are the offender, we:

- Listen graciously to the other person's view of what occurred.
- Value relationship above being right.
- Ask the Lord for His perspective on the situation and repent as needed.

- Humbly ask the other person for forgiveness, honoring his or her perceptions.
- Speak words of life and affirmation, treating the other person as we would like to be treated.
- Make restitution as needful and appropriate.

If nothing is resolved one on one, we take it to another level within the church, a company of priests—not to the outside world (See Matthew 5:23,24, Mark 11:25, Matthew 18:15-18). Paul criticized the Corinthians because they were taking one another to court before unbelievers (1 Corinthians 6:1-8). God has called some people to be Christian mediators, helping people work out their differences so we don't display them before the world.

Unity is very important. David said that a priestly anointing comes upon us collectively as we come into unity with one another (Psalm 133:1-2). That unity will bring blessing and positive changes to the society around us as the prayer of Jesus is answered:

> ...*that they may all be one; even as You, Father, are in Me and I in You, that they also may be in us, so that the world may believe that You sent me.* —John 17:21

There was unity in the upper room when the Holy Spirit came in power. He changed the weak, failure-prone disciples into mighty men and women of God filled with authority and power who turned their world upside down. The peace in them infected their world.

Let's help people be one today so the world may believe.

SETTLE DISPUTES WITH THE WORLD

We can also settle disputes in the spirit realm when the enemy uses non-believers to come against us.

My friend Regena was sued by a woman who claimed huge medical damages following a minor rear-end accident, in which there was no apparent damage to either car. A medical evaluation ruled there was less impact on the woman than if she was in a bumper car. Since Regena was also dealing with some serious unrelated health challenges, the enemy energized her fears with many sleepless nights and torment. "What if we lose all we have? What can we do?"

She was familiar with Ephesians 6:13, "*Therefore, take up the full armor of God, so that you will be able to resist in the evil day, and having done everything, to stand firm.*" Stand where? Stand doing what? There must be something more she could do. It's amazing how pain can be a launching place to new revelation and intercession.

Regena refused to become bitter toward the woman. Instead she said to the enemy, "I just want you to know that you have made this woman a target of my prayers." She also prayed, "Lord, give her more of what you intended for her when You died on the cross."

Ephesians 2:6 says that we are seated with Christ in heavenly places. This is a present reality. One day she had a vision of herself in a court room, and Jesus was her attorney. "We were presenting the case to the Most Supreme Judge of the Most Supreme Court— God, who was wearing a black robe. The jury was the great cloud of witnesses mentioned in Hebrews 12:1. There were written legal documents that Jesus had already prepared. All I had to do as the junior legal assistant was present them to the Judge. Then Jesus asked me, 'If you were to receive as much harassment from a flesh and blood person as you do from the enemy, what would you do?'

"I knew He already had the answer, but I said, 'We're filing a restraining order on the enemy!' Then Jesus handed me the previously prepared papers."

Note, Jesus didn't tell her what needed to happen or show her what was already written on the papers. He engaged in dialog with her, asking questions until the answer became clear. He was teaching her to step into a new realm of authority in Him.

"When I marched up and gave the papers to the Judge, He immediately pounded His gavel and pronounced, 'Done.'

"Later, when the enemy tried to bring it up, I said, 'it's been done. You don't have a right to do this to me! It's illegal. I have a restraining order. After this you have to face the Judge!'"

She also knew she was to celebrate before she had the answer. Praise Him now!

Not long after, the case was settled out of court. The woman received from the insurance company a tenth of what she had originally asked, and Regena's family was not adversely affected.

God gets amazing mileage out of the situations that have hurt us. This woman got marked with an "X," "blessings go here," and probably received more prayer than she ever had in her life. Regena learned more of the faithfulness and miracle working power of God, and received greater revelation of His ways that she now uses to encourage others. She also stepped into a new level of authority.

I wonder how many legal documents have already been prepared in heaven, and the Most Supreme Judge already has gavel in hand ready to pronounce, "Done!" He's waiting for us to step into our authority and declare, "Kingdom COME! God's will BE DONE on earth even as it is in heaven!"

Whatever you permit will be permitted,
whatever you do not permit will not be permitted.

—Matthew 16:19; 18:18 NIV

PAUSE & PONDER...

1. To be peace-enforcers, we must learn to walk in peace in every situation. Meditate on the following scriptures. Ask the Lord to give you revelation. How does changing your thought patterns affect your peace?

    Rejoice in the Lord always; again I will say, rejoice! Let your gentle spirit be known to all men. The Lord is near. Be anxious for nothing, but in everything by prayer and supplication with thanksgiving let your requests be made known to God.

    And the peace of God, which surpasses all comprehension, will guard your hearts and your minds in Christ Jesus.

    Finally, brethren, whatever is true, whatever is honorable, whatever is right, whatever is pure, whatever is lovely, whatever is of good repute, if there is any excellence and if anything worthy of praise, dwell on these things. The things you have learned and received and heard and seen in me, practice these things, and the God of peace will be with you. —Philippians 4:4-9

2. Are there any disputes the Lord wants you to settle? If so, ask Him for revelation on how He would like you to do that.

    Internal disputes with the enemy

    Disputes with one another

    Disputes with the world

---

[1] **5 R's of Forgiveness** in back of book shows all the principles we have learned in a more concise, easily understood format.

≈ 26 ≈
A Heart for Israel

It is as vivid in my mind today as it was when I sat as a young girl in our high school history class and watched films from World War II. The scenes are forever etched in my mind as Jews were loaded into box cars and taken to the death camps. Man's cruelty to man is truly unimaginable!

At that time God implanted within me a heart for Israel, although I had never heard anything about it from anyone in my circle of family, friends or church. I know it was a supernatural touch from God.

I firmly believe that God has also called us to **settle disputes on behalf of Israel.**

A while back I reread Jeremiah 13, where the Lord tells Jeremiah to go buy himself a linen waistband and put it around his waist. So he did.

This time as I read I put myself in the story. What would I have thought? "Shopping! Yea! I get to buy something new!"

I would eagerly say to my close friends, as I pointed to my stylin' new belt, "Do you like it?" Then I'd take a quick little spin to let them get the full effect. Okay, I'm a girl, and this is my illustration, so guys, work with me!

But then the Lord told Jeremiah to take the waistband he bought and go hide it in a crevice of the rock by the Euphrates River.

Now I am thinking, "Wait, wait! This is my new belt, and you want me to go bury it?" I do not like this so well.

But Jeremiah obeyed. Then some time later the Lord told Jeremiah to dig up the waistband. He did, but discovered it was totally ruined.

"My beautiful belt!" I would cry with a pout and a sigh.

Then the Lord tells Jeremiah the belt represents what is going to happen to the house of Israel and Judah because of their sin.

I teach classes on hearing God's voice, so I thought this was a wonderful illustration. God may speak something to us, and we, like Jeremiah, may think, "God really loves me, look at this beautiful new belt He wants me to have." But when God speaks further, we discover it has nothing to do with us, but everything to do with His plans and purposes for others. We may spend time grieving over ruined belts, when God wants us to hear His heart.

Great story. I filed it away in my memory banks, and made a note for the next time I taught a class.

A month later a friend and I went to Spokane for a conference. While walking toward the Convention Center I felt my necklace come undone, so I immediately stopped to catch it. The chain was there but the pendant was gone. I looked all around on the ground, shook out my clothing, and retraced my steps several times. I prayed. I have learned to not allow the enemy to steal from me, so I commanded him to give it back. Nothing changed.

It was gone!

Now, with most of my necklaces I may have been disappointed, but I would have let it go. This, however, was a very special pendant! It was a beautiful gold simile of the high priest's breastplate that had twelve stones, representing each of the tribes of Israel. I purchased it in Israel a couple months earlier as a reminder to pray for the lost sheep of the house of Israel. At the time I wrestled with the cost, because it was much more than I would normally spend on a piece of jewelry for myself, but I felt I was to pay the price.

Now it was gone! I did grieve. "Lord, I don't understand! I bought it because I felt like You asked me to. Why did this happen?"

Then I heard the Lord gently speak to me, "Marilyn, you bought it to remind you to pray for the lost sheep of the house of Israel. Now you know how I feel. They're lost."

The story of Jeremiah and his belt now made even more sense to me. It wasn't about me at all. The Lord goes on to say that even as the waistband clings to the waist of a man, He made Israel and Judah cling to Him, "*I did this so that they would be my people and bring fame, praise, and honor to me. However, they wouldn't listen."* Jeremiah 13:11 GW). He then instructed Jeremiah to tell them, *"If you won't listen, I will cry secretly over your arrogance. I will cry bitterly, and my eyes will flow with tears because the LORD'S flock will be taken captive."* (verse 17).

Do you hear God's heart? "I want to hold this people close to Me. I desire to give them fame and praise and honor, but I can't because they won't listen to me. I weep in secret, will you weep with me? Will you cry out for them to be found?"

God is not finished with Israel. They are still very much on His heart. God wants to bless all nations of the earth through them, including those who now call themselves their enemies. Ephesians 2:11-18 says that we have access to Jesus Christ because of them. The Jews are part of our spiritual family. Paul says in Romans 11 that the Jews were rejected for a season because of their unbelief, but that season is coming to an end:

I say then, they did not stumble so as to fall, did they? May it never be! But by their transgression salvation has come to the Gentiles, to make them jealous... For I do not want you, brethren, to be uninformed of this mystery--so that you will not be wise in your own estimation--that a partial hardening has happened to Israel until the fullness of the Gentiles has come in.
— Romans 11:11,25

For thousands of years they have been rejected and despised because the enemy knows they still have destiny to be fulfilled in God's plan. He is still trying to destroy them through the surrounding nations and godless teachings that God has forever rejected Israel and Christians have totally replaced them.

Let's settle that dispute in the heavenlies as we intercede for our brothers and sisters. Let's pray that we will be so filled with the Presence and power of God that they will become envious to know Jesus, the Messiah who has come to restore them to the Father. Let's partner with Him in bringing His lost sheep home.

We can't always settle disputes, but we can tune into God's voice and do what He asks us to do. Let's be peace enforcers so together we can walk fully in God's anointing released through unity, and see lives and communities changed and set free from captivity.

Beyond all these things put on love, which is the perfect bond of unity. —Colossians 3:14

PAUSE & PONDER…

1. In Genesis 12:2-3, God said to Abraham, *"I will make you a great nation, And I will bless you, And make your name great; And so you shall be a blessing; And I will bless those who bless you, And the one who curses you I will curse. And in you all the families of the earth will be blessed."* Have you ever cursed Israel or the Jews? If so, ask the Lord to forgive you.

    Ask the Lord to bring you opportunities to bless Israel, and the ability to recognize them when they come.

    Thank God that we have been grafted into Abraham's family, and these same blessings flow to us and through us to others.

2. If you have not done so before, ask the Lord to implant His heart for Israel in yours. Listen to His voice, see with His eyes, and feel His emotions. Write down what you experience. Now ask Him to give you His heart for the Church.

    We're in this together!

27

A Healer of Others

In our role as priests unto the Lord we are not only to be peace-keepers, but healers. Let me quote Deuteronomy 21:5 again, *"Then the priests, the sons of Levi, shall come near, for the LORD your God has chosen them to serve Him and to bless in the name of the LORD; and every dispute and every assault shall be settled by them."*

Priests were to settle disputes **AND assaults**. "Assault" is translated as a blow, wound, disease, infection, or blemish. Priests would examine wounds, apply medicine, and declare people cleansed and healed. We also have this assignment.

The former priests lived and served in a system that would come to an end. Sin was merely postponed year after year. Jesus became a high priest after the order of Melchizedek, an *everlasting* priesthood. He was sacrificed once and for all, and now intercedes continually for us.[1] It is under this royal priesthood that we serve, not because we have met any human requirements or have the proper earthly ancestry, but because we have power that comes from the life of Christ within us which cannot be destroyed. As sons and daughters of the King, and His representatives on the earth, we have access to all the kingdom protection and provision through our intimate relationship with Him.

Healing is part of our provision. Jesus has done all the work. We just enforce what He has already accomplished. Jesus paid the price for our sin and sickness. He took all of our wounds and diseases upon Himself (1 Peter 2:24).

We mentioned earlier how our negative emotions can adversely affect our health. The long-term effects of stress on our bodies, caused by relationships being out of order, need to be healed. We can help people heal when they've been wounded with the same help we've received from the Lord. We can bind up their broken hearts. We can help them recover joy, which is good medicine. As we identify with them and confess our faults and pray for one another, healing comes. We can anoint them with oil, and speak deliverance from oppression. We also can then declare them healed of their wounds, diseases, infections, or blemishes, whether they are emotional, spiritual, or physical.

God wants us to enter into a new place of faith, and believe that it has already been done! This requires a renewing of our minds, which takes time, as we daily choose to believe that what God says is true.

Even as the priests would examine a person's body to see if sickness was gone, we examine the once broken body of Jesus and see that He is now alive and well. There is no bitterness, sickness or disease in Him. And we abide IN Him! Therefore, these things have no place in us either. Jesus said, "It is finished!" It is true in heaven, we declare it on earth!

When Jesus sent out the disciples He said:

"...as you go, preach, saying, 'The kingdom of heaven is at hand.' Heal the sick, raise the dead, cleanse the lepers, cast out demons. Freely you received, freely give." — Matthew 10:7-8

Following the resurrection Jesus reaffirmed this commission. He told the disciples to go into all the world and preach good news to all creation. He then promised that signs would accompany their preaching:

...in My name they will cast out demons, they will speak with new tongues; they will pick up serpents, and if they drink any deadly poison, it will not hurt them; they will lay hands on the sick, and they will recover. — Mark 16:17-18

Then they went out and did it! Healing is not only possible, it is our mandate! We are to confirm the word of God with His power manifested on earth.

The biggest obstacles are in our mind, not in the power of God. I am aware that many people doubt that God does heal today, despite abundant evidence to the contrary. Some beliefs have been adjusted and taught according to what hasn't happened instead of the truth of God's word. We may be offended at God because in the past we asked Him to heal us or someone else and it didn't occur. In this book my goal is not to answer all the questions you may have about the prayers that weren't answered. I can only declare to you the truth that God is always good and He still heals. I personally have experienced miraculous healing in my own life, and witnessed it in the lives of many others.

Jesus said we would do the same things He did. His Hebrew name, Yeshua, means "Jehovah saves." The word "saves" means deliverance, victory, and prosperity for our entire self: body, soul, and spirit. Romans 10:9-10 says, *"that if you confess with your mouth Jesus as Lord, and believe in your heart that God raised Him from the dead, you will be saved; for with the heart a person believes, resulting in righteousness, and with the mouth he confesses, resulting in salvation."* "Saved" here is the Greek word "sozo," which means to deliver, protect, and make whole, and "salvation" is "soteria," which also means deliverance, health, and salvation.

Take a look at that scripture again. Salvation comes, deliverance and health come, as we believe (changing our thoughts to align with God's words and thoughts) and confess with our mouths what He says to be true. If Jesus still saves, He also still heals and delivers. It's part of the package. Healing is part of our inheritance, as much as salvation from sin. True, not everyone may get healed this side of heaven, but we can grow in our ability and faith to believe for miracles, even as we can increase stamina and strength through physical exercise.

We may be waiting for God to come and zap us with His power, but He's waiting for us! He's already sent His Holy Spirit to dwell in us—the same Spirit that was in Jesus Christ and the early disciples. It's time to step out in faith and use it. As we learn to abide in Him and are continually filled with His Spirit and joy, as we become Presence-based rather than performance-based, more concerned about having the Presence of the King with us than having man approve of us, faith will grow, and we will begin to see healings and miracles happen.

People are being miraculously healed and raised from the dead in many parts of our country and world. Why not here, why not now? It *is* time.

> *… he who believes in Me, the works that I do,*
> *he will do also; and greater works than these he will do…*
>   —John 14:12

ᔧ◆ᔨ

PAUSE & PONDER…

1. Do you have any past experiences, preconceived notions or beliefs that rule out healing and miracles? If so, what are they? Ask the Lord to show you if your beliefs or perception of experiences are in disagreement with the word of God.

2. What does it mean to be Presence-based rather than performance-based when it comes to the miraculous?

3. Pray, "Lord, I ask you to renew my mind to believe that I can do the things that You did, because Your Spirit dwells in me. I accept Your mandate. Open Your Word to me in new ways, and bring into my life people and resources that will help me grow in faith to believe for the miraculous. Teach me how to pray IN the Holy Spirit and rightly represent You and Your kingdom on earth in my attitudes and demonstrations of Your power and love."

---

[1] See footnote 1 at end of Chapter 14.

[2] See 2 Corinthians 1:4, Psalm 147:3, Isaiah 61:1, Proverbs 17:22, James 5:14-16, Mark 6:13, Luke 13:11-13, Luke 4:40

[3] See Matthew 9:35; Mark 16:15-18; John 14:12; Acts 2:38-39; 3:17; 4:28-31; 10:38. There are many other scriptures that could be mentioned.

❧ 28 ❧
ℒo You
See the Army?

After the seventy years of captivity were fulfilled, God moved in the heart of Cyrus, the king of Persia, to allow the children of Israel to return to their own land.[1] When released they sang this song:

> ...When the LORD brought back the captive ones of Zion, We were like those who dream. Then our mouth was filled with laughter And our tongue with joyful shouting; Then they said among the nations, "The LORD has done great things for them." The LORD has done great things for us; We are glad. – Psalm 126:1-3

For them it was a dream fulfilled. Jesus has a dream too. His dream is that we would be one as He and His Father are one that the world may believe in Him. He reduced all the law to two commands, "Love God," and "Love People." He wants the world to experience His love through us.

Jesus said we are the light of the world. Your light will never shine brighter than the times you choose to love when wounded or persecuted. You will become a beacon to those around you who face difficulties, when they see the grace, joy and love displayed through you."

Years ago I awoke from a dream of a large mass of people on a football field at half-time. They all had different colors of flags and clothing. Some were very plain, while others were bright and flamboyant. There was tremendous discord on the field as everyone beat those around them with their flags. The people in the stands were shocked by what was going on, but eventually lost interest and began milling around. Then an interesting thing happened.

A conductor stood up and called everyone on the field to order. Fighting stopped, colors were rearranged, and there began to emerge on the field a picture — the face of Jesus. Now the people in the stands took notice and watched to see what would happen next.

Could this be the generation when the world would see Jesus in us — when they would know us by our love? Or must we wait for yet another generation?

When I married Doug after several years of being single, I had this familiar song played on the piano as I walked down the aisle.

> Jesus loves me this I know
> For the Bible tells me so
> Little ones to Him belong
> They are weak but He is strong
> Yes Jesus loves me, Yes Jesus loves me
> Yes Jesus loves me, the Bible tells me so[2]

Not everyone caught the melody, but tears trickled down the faces of a few of those who knew my struggles. The little song learned in Sunday School may have seemed childish to some, but it was a truth embedded in my heart. You see, it's not just the Bible that tells me so. God's people show me so:

- God loves me through Doug. I continually see the love of my Father in his eyes.
- God loves me through those who did not reject me when it would have been easy to judge.
- God loves me through those who have forgiven my sins and shortcomings.

Believe that God loves you too. Receive His love in those intimate appointment times with Him, and then give it away. Experience His gentle touch as you walk in relationships with others. Let Him fill your thoughts throughout the day. I'm sure you're like me; I don't want to miss our day of visitation by Jesus to a world that is desperate for His love.

Jesus walked among the Pharisees but they didn't recognize Him. They knew the Scriptures, but they didn't know Him, because they forgot how to love.

I pray that there would be about our lives irrefutable evidence in every court of the world, "You can't deny it, we know you love Jesus, because you love people. The kind of love you display can only come from knowing Him."

May we hear the pounding of the gavel, and hear the verdict, "Guilty as charged," pronounced with assurance.

The early disciples did. They received the **authority** to do the things that Jesus did that day in the locked room, but on the day of Pentecost they received the **power** to fully walk in that authority. The once frightened, huddled few stood up boldly in the streets of Jerusalem and declared who Jesus was, and three thousand were redeemed in one day! They were known as the ones who turned the world upside down. They had been judged as uneducated and untrained men; but they amazed religious rulers who recognized they had been with Jesus (Acts 4:13).

This same power is available to us today, not through a one-time experience, but a continual infilling of the Holy Spirit. Jesus said that out of our innermost being would flow rivers of living water. Ezekiel 47 says the river brings life wherever it goes and it actually gets deeper the further it travels from the house of the Lord.

Revival and transformation come when we stop waiting for revival and have it. I want to give you some good news. **Today is the day of visitation.** "...*Now is the time of God's favor, now is the day of salvation*" (2 Corinthians 6:2). Jesus is here; the Holy Spirit is here. As Gypsy Smith, an evangelist of the late 1800's and early 1900's said, if you want revival, go into your bedroom, kneel before the Lord, draw a circle in chalk around you, and pray that God will start a revival in that circle.

When people get filled with the Holy Spirit, leave the safety of the upper room or church building, and allow Him to flow out on all those around them, lives will be changed and cities will be transformed. Such a people cannot be confined in the prisons of the world. There is a freedom and joy inside that will defy persecution.

Jubilee begins in our hearts, as we set our own captives free, and then go *"about doing good and healing all who were oppressed by the devil,"* for God is with you (Acts 10:38).

My friend...

- It is time to dream again.
- It is time to blow the trumpet and declare that God really is THAT good, and He's in a good mood!
- It is time to proclaim liberty to all those who are in captivity.
- It is time to buy back those who have been taken captive to other nations.
- It is time to return to the land of our inheritance, to build again the waste places, and raise up age-old foundations.
- It is time we were known as those who repair the broken walls of people's lives and our cities, and those who restore our streets so people can live in freedom and safety (Isaiah 58:12).
- It is time to gather again in families, and produce children who look just like their Father!
- It is time to restore everything to its rightful owner, Jesus.

  "For by Him all things were created, both in the heavens and on earth, visible and invisible, whether thrones or dominions or rulers or authorities – all things have been created through Him and for him." – Colossians 1:16

- It is time *"TO TURN THE HEARTS OF THE FATHERS BACK TO THE CHILDREN, and the disobedient to the attitude of the righteous, so as to make ready a people prepared for the Lord."* – Luke 1:17

How do we do these things? I could give you my theories and methods I've learned or heard from others. However, we've had enough of formulas that may have worked at one time, but now are devoid of power. God's Word and history teach us that each battle requires a new strategy direct from the Lord. Yesterday's method may not work. He wants to infuse fresh life into all that we do.

In a time when the world's kingdoms and economies are shaking He wants to give us the currency of heaven, which will always be more than enough for what He places in our hearts. He wants us to be totally dependent upon Him, so we can do more than we ever thought possible, and He can receive greater glory as His kingdom is increased.

Each of us must get quiet long enough to hear God for ourselves on His strategy for today, in this time, in this place. It is not about our performance. It is seeing the laugh wrinkles around His eyes, and His mouth turned up in a smile. It is daily walking with an awareness of His love and presence, and doing what we see Him do. We may not yet see clearly, but we do know:

- The power of the Holy Spirit will be released through those who are filled with passion and desire for Jesus above all else.
- The gospel of the kingdom will be preached with simplicity and experienced with profound joy.
- Release from every form of bondage will take place in supernatural ways as the kingdom is released and justice restored.
- The love and compassion of Christ will be expressed through us in tangible ways that will melt hearts.
- Many workers will be needed to gather in the harvest.

Jesus did not say to pray for the harvest. The harvest is ready. He said to ask for workers (See Matthew 9:35-38).

I have a recurring vision of a group of people coming over the horizon — they are prisoners of war and missing in action coming home. They are lame, blind, and broken, but they're coming home. Unfortunately, many of these have been wounded in our churches;

they've been disconnected from the body. Some have lost faith entirely. Others still feel they love God, but want nothing to do with God's people because of the wounds they've received. Others sit as dead men in our churches week after week. Will you intercede for them? Will you stand up and prophesy as Ezekiel did over the valley of dry bones:

> *"...He said to me, 'Son of man, can these bones live?' And I answered, 'O Lord GOD, You know.'*
>
> *Again He said to me, 'Prophesy over these bones and say to them, "O dry bones, hear the word of the LORD...I will cause breath to enter you that you may come to life. I will put sinews on you, make flesh grow back on you, cover you with skin and put breath in you that you may come alive; and you will know that I am the LORD."'*
>
> *"...As I prophesied, there was a noise, and behold, a rattling; and the bones came together, bone to its bone. And I looked, and behold, sinews were on them, and flesh grew and skin covered them; but there was no breath in them. Then He said to me, 'Prophesy to the breath... "Thus says the Lord GOD, 'Come from the four winds, O breath, and breathe on these slain, that they come to life.' So I prophesied as He commanded me, and the breath came into them, and they came to life and stood on their feet, an exceedingly great army."* —Ezekiel 37:1-10

Can you hear the rattling? Can you feel the wind? Will you love people back to life? Will you give them a fresh start? Will you listen to the Father and then speak His words of encouragement that breathe fresh hope into them? Will you declare their future in Christ instead of their past sin? Will you release the dreams in others so their mouths can be filled with laughter, and tongues be filled with shouts of joy?

I believe there is a mighty army among the dry bones who will step into place, Jew and Gentile alike—passionate lovers who will speak God's heart rather than their own judgments. An army who will declare with authority, "Your sins are forgiven!" A company of priests who with irrepressible joy and unity will go throughout the land declaring the kingdom of God is here and setting the captives free. A people who will do the greater things that Jesus promised — workers who will gather in the harvest.

Are you ready? Will you join them? We can do it together. The world is waiting.

The loved forgive.

The forgiven love.

It is time.

PAUSE & PONDER...

1. Spend some time worshipping and praising the Lord. Then ask Him to fill you afresh with His Holy Spirit, the breath of God, so you can have the power to walk in the authority He has given you. Give Him thanks, then spend some time receiving His life into you.

2. Pray over the list above where it says, "It is time to..." What stirs in your heart? What has God uniquely equipped you to do?

3. Ask the Lord, "What now? How do I put what I've learned into practice?"

---

[1] See Jeremiah 29:7-14, Ezra 1-2

[2] "Jesus Loves Me," by Anna B. Warner (verse 1) and David Rutherford McGuire (verse 2, 3), William B. Bradbury (chorus and music), 1860-62

Epilogue

What now? Your past is gone. You no longer have to waste time thinking about what "coulda, shoulda, woulda been." Jubilee is here! TODAY you get a fresh start. You have a bright future of hope ahead of you. What will fill the pages of your life from here on out? How will you display the glory of the Lord? How many lives will you affect as the love of the Lord flows through you?

Dare to dream. Dare to believe. Dare to go and do!

God has chosen you to be part of His royal priesthood,
a people for His own possession,
so that you may proclaim the excellencies of Him
who has called you out of darkness into His marvelous light.
You once were not a people,
but now you are the people of God;
you had not received mercy,
but now you have received mercy.
Therefore, may the Lord direct your hearts into
God's love and Christ's perseverance.
May the Lord make your love increase and overflow
for each other and for everyone else…May He strengthen
your hearts so that you will be blameless and holy in the presence
of our God and Father when our Lord Jesus comes
with all his holy ones.

The grace of our Lord Jesus Christ be with you all.[1]

---

[1] See 1 Peter 2:9-10, 2 Thessalonians 3:5,18 1 Thessalonians 3:12-13

The Acorn, Take 2

You can't see it, the little acorn in my pocket.
I feel the smooth nut and textured cap,
As my fingers gently caress it.
At times during the day, often as I can,
I remember God's promises and give thanks again,
Then I bring it out and before my eyes
The cap comes off, branches grow,
And leaves spread far and wide—
This tree of grace and beauty transcends the works of man!
"It's impossible! How, can it be?"
I cry on the one hand.
And on the other, I'm filled with excitement, joy and glee
As Faith, Hope and Love, my treasured friends,
Come out to play with me.
On the stage we've created high in the limbs
Over and over we recount our thankfulness to Him.
He's worked for good each experience, joy, and pain,
And shown His grace and faithfulness
Time and time again.
As we do my roots grow deep
And branches reach high in praise,
For nothing is impossible,
He'll do just what He says.
My heart beats swift, and by faith I see
In the small little acorn
God's image formed in me.
And I'm filled with hope that I'll be someday
A mighty oak of righteousness
His glory to display.

—Marilyn Hume

Journaling Tips

Journaling is a great tool for growing in our relationship with God. In journaling we:

- Learn to distinguish God's words from our own or the voice of the enemy. It's amazing to go back and read a section we have journaled and see how God clearly spoke. Other times it is easy to identify that some thoughts come from our own reasoning.
- Allow Jesus to be our teacher as our thoughts are yielded to His.
- Receive wisdom and guidance in our decision processes.
- Allow the Holy Spirit to remind us of what Jesus said in the Word.
- Learn more of who God is, His ways, and His thoughts.
- Learn to separate truth from error.
- Hear His heart for us and others.
- Receive insight and direction on how to live a supernatural life.
- Learn how to pray in agreement with His will.
- Have fun! There is nothing more exciting than hearing God's voice and responding to him!

There are many ways to journal, and over time you will find what works best for you. **Choose a quiet, comfortable place**, with few distractions. It is sometimes helpful to have some worship music playing softly in the background, preferably without any words, so your mind is not drawn to the lyrics.

Before you start, **ask the Lord to cleanse you** from:

1. Any unconfessed sin.
2. Any reasoning and judgments of what you think about an issue. You may pray something like this:

"Father, I submit my will, my thoughts, and my judgments to Yours. I will not listen to my own flesh or any spirit but the Spirit of God."

Now **believe that God wants to speak to you.** Jesus said, *"My sheep hear My voice, and I know them, and they follow me"* (John 10: 27).

Jeremiah 29:11-13 says, *"I know the plans that I have for you,' declares the LORD, 'plans for welfare and not for calamity to give you a future and a hope. Then you will call upon Me and come and pray to me, and I will listen to you. You will seek Me and find Me when you search for Me with all your heart."*

Listen to Jeremiah 33:3, *"Call to Me and I will answer you, and I will tell you great and mighty things, which you do not know."*

God wants to speak to YOU!

Thank the Lord that you can hear His voice. Give Him praise for who He is. Let your praise be more than words, but engage your body, soul, and spirit in worship. As Graham Cooke says, "Give thanks until you become thanks."

When you're ready to continue, **write down a question** you want to ask the Lord. Then **sit and wait quietly. Put down what comes to mind.** Don't immediately try to examine whether it was from the Lord. For now just write, with your thoughts focused toward him.

Ask more questions as necessary.

Be honest about your thoughts and feelings, and allow Him to respond back to you.

It's helpful to have a Bible and concordance handy, in case the Lord brings any scriptures to your mind.

Some questions you might ask are:
- "What would you like to say to me today, Lord?"
- "Is there a particular section of scripture you would like to show me this morning?"
- "How do I apply this verse to my life?"

- "I feel like I'm having difficulty hearing You. Are there any blocks in me?"
- "What would You have me pray about?"
- "Is there someone on Your heart You would like me to intercede for today?"
- "What's on your heart today, Lord?"
- "Lord, what would You have me do in this situation?"
- "Where were You when this happened, Lord?"
- "Is that You, Lord?"

The possibilities are limitless. Many times God speaks in key words and phrases, rather than full sentences. A lot of what you hear will be a combination of His voice and yours. But you will get better at distinguishing the difference. His voice is always in agreement with His Word and His character. God is good; His voice brings peace and assurance, not condemnation.

You may also want to add artwork to your journaling. If God gives you a picture in your mind, use your imagination. Any small child will show you that your imagination is God-given. Become child-like again. What do you see? Look for detail. What is God saying by the picture? What does He want you to know? Sketch it, then add color or whatever your heart desires. Don't look for perfection. Stick figures are great! Have fun and release that which is in you. Let your creativity flow! God is the creator, and He loves to release creativity in us!

5 R's of Forgiveness

I will RECALL
- What forgiveness is and what it isn't:
  - It is not saying that what you did is okay.
  - It is not removing consequences of your actions, but God gets to choose those consequences not me.
  - It is not trust. Trust has to be earned in process.
  - It is not reconciliation. That is only possible through repentance and restoration of relationship.
  - It is giving up my right to get even with you.
  - It is caring for you enough to confront your actions if needed.
  - It is caring for me enough to set up appropriate boundaries if you are unwilling to change.
- What I am forgiving specifically.
- What I have lost.

I will REPENT
- For my lack of faith and trust in the justice, mercy, and goodness of God.
- For allowing my judgments of you to steal my peace and joy.
- For holding bitterness against you.

I will RELEASE
- My grief, anger, and hurt over what I have lost.
- My judgments of you, and allow God to be your judge.
- Blessings on you in my thoughts and actions.

I will RECEIVE
- God's forgiveness, healing and love.

I will REMEMBER
- To give God thanks for:
  - His faithfulness in the past.
  - The awesome things He has promised for my future.

HAS THIS BOOK BLESSED YOU?
If so, let us know by e-mailing us at:

itistime@bethbiri.com

About the Author...

Marilyn Hume has been a staff pastor at East Hill Church in Gresham, Oregon for many years, and is now expressing her passion and gifts through Beth-biri House of Creativity. She teaches locally and internationally. Marilyn and her husband Doug have four children and six grandchildren.

If you would like to know more about Beth-biri, visit:

www.bethbiri.com

Marilyn is available for speaking engagements and inter-active training seminars where she helps people experiment and gain new skills in hearing God, prophetic prayer, intercession, worship, and releasing creativity in a safe environment. You may contact her at:

marilyn@bethbiri.com

You are God's house!

Made in the USA